THE
BEGINNER'S
GUIDE TO
DIVINATION

THE BEGINNER'S GUIDE TO DIVINATION

how to reveal the future, from crystal balls and
palm reading to tarot, runes, tea leaves,
and more

KIRSTEN RIDDLE

CICO BOOKS

This book is dedicated to all the wise, wonderful, witchy women out there
who use their intuition every day.

Published in 2026 by CICO Books
An imprint of Ryland Peters & Small Ltd
20–21 Jockey's Fields   1452 Davis Bugg Road
London WC1R 4BW   Warrenton, NC 27589
www.rylandpeters.com
Email: euregulations@rylandpeters.com

10 9 8 7 6 5 4 3 2 1

A CIP record for this book is available from the British Library.
US Library of Congress CIP data has been applied for.

ISBN: 978-1-80065-590-4

Printed in China

Desk editor: Imogen Valler-Miles
Senior designer: Emily Breen
Art director: Sally Powell
Creative director: Leslie Harrington
Head of production: Patricia Harrington
Publishing manager: Carmel Edmonds

The authorised representative in the EEA is
Authorised Rep Compliance Ltd.,
Ground Floor. 71 Lower Baggot Street,
Dublin, D01 P593, Ireland
www.arccompliance.com

MIX
Paper | Supporting
responsible forestry
FSC
www.fsc.org
FSC® C008047

Safety note:

Neither the author nor the publisher can be held responsible
for any claim arising out of the general information and
practices provided in this book. While the use of essential oils,
herbs, incense, and particular practices may refer to healing
benefits, they are not intended to replace diagnosis of illness
or ailments, or healing or medicine. Always consult your
doctor or other health professional in the case of illness.
Essential oils are very powerful and potentially toxic if used
too liberally. Follow the advice given on the label and never
use the oils neat on bare skin, or if pregnant.

The safe and proper use of fire, candles, incense, matches, and
lighters is the sole responsibility of the person using them. Do
not leave a burning flame unattended. Never burn a flame on
or near anything that might catch fire. Keep fire out of the
reach of children and pets.

Contents

Introduction

Since the dawn of millennia, humans have sought answers to life's big questions through divination—the art of predicting the future. We have pondered and prophesized and looked to the heavens for divine guidance, petitioning the relevant pantheon to bless us with a sign that would reflect future events. We have studied the stars and planets, seeking inspiration from their nightly dance across the sky, even looking to meteorological elements for inspiration, believing that a sudden change of weather, such as a storm or a hurricane, could be a message from the gods. We have taken our lead from specific environmental changes and watched the movements and behaviors of the creatures that we share the Earth with, in the hope of receiving daily direction and finding answers to some of the most pertinent questions.

Prehistoric people examined the entrails of birds and mammals, paying particular attention to the size and shape of the liver. This early form of divination might seem gory to contemporary eyes, but our predecessors used what they had to hand, in a bid to make sense of the world around them. This practice, known as hepatoscopy, was also popular with some of the more recent Ancients, such as the Egyptians and the Romans, although they also favored dream divination, believing that their nightly visions were communicated from the deities.

The Sumerians and Babylonians of ancient Mesopotamia (a historic region of present-day Iraq) preferred looking up at the stars. They saw the sky as a magical canopy, a dense backdrop that could reveal future events. A collection of tablets from the second century BCE, known as the Enuma Anu Enlil, records those first forays and their importance in predicting fate. The ancient Greeks also loved to dabble in astrology and used a range of tools to divine the future. Prediction was a key part of their daily life and held great sway with the leaders of the time. They employed seers and oracles—the most famous being the Oracle at Delphi—to commune with the gods and deliver prophecies.

Jump forward in time to the tarot—a carefully curated and colorful collection of cards that emerged from Italy during the Renaissance, with images so powerful they strike a chord with the imagination and trigger the psyche at a much deeper level. A parlor game or the key to destiny? The question remains, but one thing is certain—the symbols within each deck reveal the twists and turns of fate with succinct precision.

There are those who believe divination should be resigned to the realms of mystics and circus travelers, but it's just as prevalent and popular today as it has always been. We have the same questions we always had; the desire to know the unknown, to delve beneath the surface, and to understand why things happen the way they do is universal. As the wheel of each year moves on, we become more attuned to nature, seeking the connection that our ancestors had with the world around them. Our innate intuition, which has taken a back seat for generations, is ready to surface and we are open and willing to listen to those subtle shifts in atmosphere and what they might mean for us.

And so here we are, at the start of your divinatory journey and there is much to see and do! Divination is a huge umbrella, covering a plethora of techniques, skills, and practices. Each chapter in this book outlines a different type of divination. You'll learn about each specific practice, where it comes from, and how the Ancients used it to divine the future. You'll discover what you need to prepare and get started, practical advice on honing your technique, and rituals and exercises that will improve your psychic ability and aid you in your quest. Tips at the end of each chapter will enhance what you have learned, should you want to take your knowledge a step further.

Most importantly, this book offers a starting point for those fascinated by the esoteric arts. Whether you have an interest in divination as a whole or you want to improve your intuition and have some fun, you'll find everything you need here. So, if you're seeking a sign to spur you onward, then take a breath. Take a moment. Let the pages fall open where they will and read on. An exciting future awaits!

CHAPTER ONE

GETTING STARTED

In this chapter, you will discover the items you
need to create your psychic workspace, learn the
differences between reading for yourself and
reading for others, and practice using a pendulum,
which is one of the simplest divination tools.

Create your psychic workspace

Preparation is imperative for successful divination work, so it's worth spending the time to make sure you have everything in place before you launch into the practical side of prediction. You will need to create a psychic workspace—an area where you can practice different types of divination without being disturbed. This could be an entire room or simply a small corner. Here are some of the basic items you might need to get started and to create the perfect workspace.

Table and tablecloth

You will need a table to work on to lay cards, cast runes or sticks, and perform other intuitive readings. If the table or its surroundings are cluttered, this could block the flow of psychic energy, so make sure there is plenty of space on and around your table to arrange your tools and to sit comfortably. Some readers like to use a special tablecloth, which is usually black, to shield the space, the tools, and the reader from negative energy.

Oils and oil burner

Essential oils are a helpful addition to any psychic workspace. They aid divination by promoting a calm, relaxed atmosphere. You can burn them in an oil burner, or if you prefer, add a few drops to a small bowl of hot water and let the scented vapor fill the room. Lavender, sandalwood, and ylang ylang all have soothing properties; frankincense lifts the atmosphere and helps you tap into your higher "intuitive" self; while rosemary is a potent scent that cleanses and also promotes psychic power.

Incense

Like essential oils, incense helps by creating the perfect atmosphere for any type of divination. There is a range of scented sticks to choose from, which you can purchase from specialist stores online. It's worth trying a few before you begin your divination work to see how they make you feel.

Crystals

Crystals are the perfect companions for psychic work. They amplify and transmit energy, helping to strengthen intuitive channels, making it easier for you to pick up messages and insights. Do your research and find the right crystal for you by reading about each stone's properties. There are plenty of amazing resources online to help you with this.

Complete beginners might find it useful to invest in a piece of amethyst, which promotes the flow of psychic energy and helps to open the third eye chakra—this is the energy center associated with intuition and is located in the center of the forehead.

Candles

Candles are another tool that can be used in divination—for smoke scrying (see pages 40–41) in particular, but also as a general tool to have nearby to help focus the mind. Scented candles emit a gentle aroma that soothes and uplifts while also creating the right ambiance for readings. As with oils and incense, it's a good idea to experiment and find the right candle for the occasion. For example, if you're setting the scene, tealights work well as they're small and unobtrusive, but if you're going to be scrying as part of your reading, you might want to use a bigger candle.

Divination journal

A divination journal is essential for those who want to improve their divination skills. It can be used to reflect on your practice and to make a record of each reading. If you get into the habit of writing a few notes about each experience, you'll be able to track your progress and see what works for you. Choose a special book for this and keep it solely for prediction purposes.

Reading for yourself and for others

Most psychics start by reading for themselves in order to hone their craft before performing readings for others. If you want to develop your psychic skills, you'll probably do both, and become adept at switching roles. At the core of divination is the "reading." This includes reading a person directly or using a tool to provide clues that are deciphered to form the prediction.

The person who receives the reading is known as the "querent" because they are seeking answers about, or "querying," the future. The person who performs the reading is known as the "reader" because they are "reading" the clues. When you read for yourself, you take on both roles. Here are some tips to help you make the most of each scenario.

When you are reading for yourself

- Be honest about what you see, feel, or experience. It's easy to twist the narrative to suit your wants and needs, but try to avoid this.

- Record your findings. Even if they don't make sense to you in the current moment, write down the results of each reading so that you can refer back to them and track your progress.

- Be kind to yourself. This is a learning process and it takes time. You can't expect to be an expert overnight, so be patient and allow your skills to grow.

When you are reading for others

- Perform a cleansing ritual before each reading to clear the area of psychic residue left over from previous readings. Burn sage-scented oil or use a smudge stick made of herbs and let the scented smoke infuse the space with positive energy. Alternatively, try the practice on page 52.

- Trust your instincts. Go with what you feel and seek clarification from the querent by asking if certain feelings and insights make sense to them.

- Don't worry. If you don't receive a prediction or reading, it could be that it isn't the right time for you to receive this information, or that you're not the best fit for the querent. We connect differently with everyone; the psychic link can be strong or weak depending on the people involved.

Tune in to another person's energy

Reading from or for another person takes time and practice, but this simple exercise will help you connect with someone else's energy before you perform a reading for them.

You will need: A comfortable, quiet space for you and the querent to sit.

1   Sit opposite the querent and center yourself by taking a few long, deep breaths. Maintain eye contact as you do this.

2   Focus on your heart chakra, which is the energy center situated in the middle of your chest. As you breathe, imagine a warm, rosy glow emanating from this space. See this as a tendril of light that gets stronger and brighter with every breath.

3   Imagine the tendril of light extending directly outward, connecting you to the heart chakra of the querent. See this connection as a cord of light bringing you both together.

4   Close your eyes and feel the energy traveling along this channel—let it settle within. You might notice emotions pouring forth, you might feel aches or pains, or even have thoughts that appear alien to you. Don't worry—you're establishing a connection with the other person and picking up on how they think and feel at this moment in time.

5   You are now ready to perform the reading of your choice. When you have finished the reading, remember to disconnect from the querent by visualizing the cord of light gently fading away with every breath you take. It also helps to imagine yourself cocooned in white light as you sever the connection.

Pendulum dowsing

Pendulum dowsing is one of the simplest and easiest forms of divination. A pendulum is a psychic tool comprised of a weighted object. It is an excellent tool to practice with at the start of your divinatory journey because it can only give "yes" or "no" responses to questions. It is worth practicing with a pendulum to connect with your intuition on a basic level before exploring the other practices in the following chapters.

The weighted object that forms the pendulum can be a crystal, a stone, a metal object, such as a key, or even a bead or other type of trinket, depending on the reader's preference. The object hangs at the end of a chain, rope, or cord and when held aloft, the direction of the pendulum's swing provides "yes" or "no" answers to questions about current situations and the future. The pendulum acts as a conduit to the higher self, the intuitive side of the brain. It moves instinctively to reveal answers, acting like a transmitter and channeling a direct response from the intuition.

A pendulum can be used for a number of purposes, from answering direct questions and helping with decision-making to gaining further insight on health issues and divining energy ley lines (energy pathways that connect significant landmarks and sites across the world). Some readers also use their pendulum to find lost items.

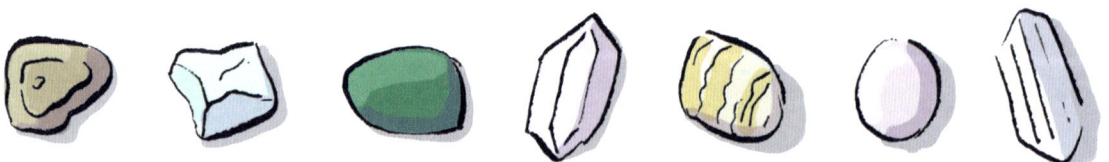

Early techniques

Pendulum dowsing was used by ancient civilizations, such as the Egyptians, Greeks, and Romans, for guidance and to predict the future. Pendulums were held aloft maps to identify promising travel routes and to divine strategic solutions in battle. They might also have been used to commune with the gods. There are mentions of pendulum dowsing in ancient Chinese texts that suggest the practice was carried out to locate precious minerals, fertile land, and sources of water.

This use of dowsing is called "water divining" and the practice became popular throughout Europe in the Middle Ages, when it was used by farmers and miners to locate underground streams and wells. Either a pendulum was used, which reacted positively when it passed over a source of water, or a forked Y-shaped piece of wood, usually hazel, holly, or willow—all renowned for their mystical properties—was carried over an area to divine its true worth. If the piece of wood quivered or moved in any way, this was a sign that water was present.

Modern dowsing equipment takes the form of a pair of L-shaped metal rods, one of which is held in each hand. The rods cross over one another or move away from one another to indicate when water is present. To this day, some water companies still use dowsing rods, alongside more modern technology, to detect water leaks.

Types of pendulum

The type of pendulum you choose depends on personal preference and your specific needs. Anything that is small and can be easily attached to a chain or cord can be used as a pendulum. Some readers like to use beads or special stones, while others prefer a piece of metal formed into a cone. Keys are especially good because they are linked to new beginnings and opportunities, and they can be helpful when trying to find lost pets—tie a piece of your pet's hair or fur around the hole at the top of the key to help connect you to your pet. Other people like to work with crystal pendulums because crystals have unique energies that can be harnessed to align with your specific questions or needs (see box below).

TOP TIP
Crystal choice

When selecting a crystal for a pendulum, consider the energies of different crystals and how they might resonate with you.

Clear quartz: Synonymous with clarity and will help to connect you to your higher self.

Rose quartz: Embodies healing energy and is perfect if you are divining illness or if you have questions relating to love.

Amethyst: An extremely spiritual stone that can help you find your higher purpose, making it ideal for bigger questions and issues.

Pendulum charging with the four elements

You will need to charge your pendulum to make it fit for purpose. Many readers who work with crystal pendulums like to bathe them in salt water to remove any negative energy, but it is entirely up to you how you charge your pendulum. Sitting with your pendulum with the intention of charging it is enough.

Below is a charging ritual that you can use with any type of pendulum, which uses the four elements—Earth, Air, Fire, and Water—to make a symbolic statement.

You will need: A small bowl of fresh water, a white tealight (white for purity) in a holder, your pendulum, a match or lighter, and some space outside on a dry and wind-free day!

1   Find a comfortable place where you can sit outside, ideally on a patch of grass or earth, and place the bowl of water and the tealight in front of you.

2   Hold your pendulum and take a minute to set your intention. For example, you could say "I create this sacred space to charge and cleanse my pendulum."

3   Place your pendulum in front of the tealight and the bowl of water.

4   Press the pendulum gently into the earth and say "By Earth, I ground you."

5   Light the tealight and say "By Fire, I cleanse you."

6   Dip your fingers into the water and sprinkle a few drops over the pendulum. Say "By Water, I purify you."

7   Take a deep breath and, as you exhale, let your breath fall over the pendulum and the tealight so that you extinguish the flame. Say "By Air, I charge you."

8   To finish, hold the pendulum in both hands, close your eyes, and visualize it bathed in pure, white light.

Establish your "yes" and "no" responses

You will need to establish a connection with your pendulum before you can begin to use it for prediction purposes. The pendulum is an extension of your psyche so it's important that you get used to handling it and reading its responses. The following exercise will help you decipher "yes" and "no" answers and strengthen the bond you have with this psychic tool.

You will need: Your pendulum and a comfortable space to sit.

1 Sit holding the pendulum in whichever hand feels natural. Hold it between your index finger and thumb, wrapping any excess chain or cord around your index finger, and let it dangle freely. As you do this, set your intention to work with the pendulum. You could say something like "I charge you as an extension of my intuition to guide and direct me."

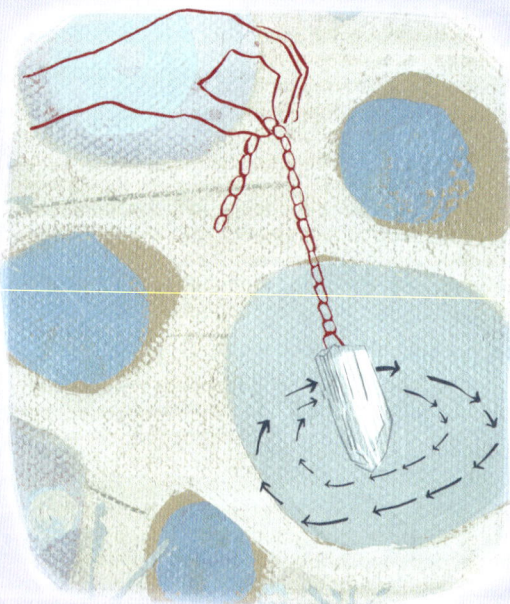

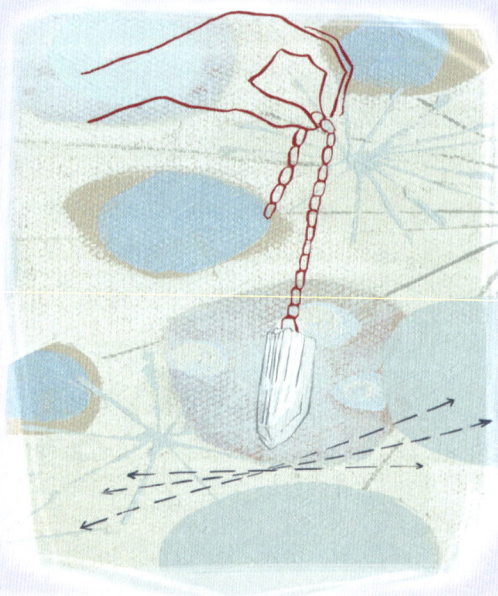

2 To find your "yes" response, relax and bring to mind a happy memory—relive it and experience those joyful emotions once more. As you do this, watch the pendulum and notice the direction it is moving in. This is your "yes" response. "Yes" answers are commonly associated with a clockwise movement, but the motion is entirely unique to you. For example, the pendulum could move back and forth instead.

3 To find your "no" response, ask a question for which you know the answer is a "no." For example, you might say "Am I a kangaroo?" Watch the pendulum move, usually in the opposite direction to the "yes" response, and make a note of its motion. This is your "no" response.

4 Double-check your pendulum's movements by asking a "yes" question, such as, "Am I human?" If you've established a strong link with your pendulum then it should revert to its natural "yes" response.

5 Practice, practice, practice. Repeat questions until you feel satisfied that you've established the right "yes" and "no" responses. Once you feel confident, you can begin to ask questions about current and future situations. Be sure to phrase your questions in a way that can only be answered with a "yes" or "no" response.

TOP TIP
Unclear responses

There will be times when your intuition wavers and you might not receive a definitive answer. In this case, your pendulum might respond with no movement or a different type of motion. When this happens, you can either repeat the question by saying "ask again," or you can take the unclear response as an indicator that things could go either way and that it's best for you to let events unfold.

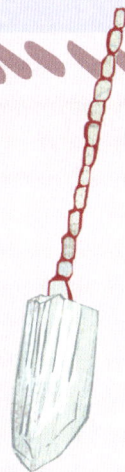

Pendulum dowsing step-by-step

1 Find the right space to work in. Try not to position yourself close to any electrical equipment that might interfere with the flow of psychic energy. Instead, find a comfortable space and turn off your cell phone, tablet, and any other technology.

2 Relaxation is key. The pendulum is a receiver, picking up messages from your intuitive mind. It only works when the channel of communication is clear so it's important to still your mind and get into a relaxed state first. This will give you the best possible chance of success. A five-minute meditation or breathing exercise before you begin can help with this; you could try the breathing ritual on page 78.

3 Know what you want to ask. It can help to prepare some questions first and write them down, but if your session is spontaneous then give yourself time to set an intention and have a clear purpose in mind. Remember to keep your questions clear and concise and make sure they can be answered with a "yes" or "no."

4 Hold the pendulum aloft in a way that works for you and begin asking your questions. If you're struggling to get any kind of response, don't force things. Pendulum dowsing can be affected by a number of factors. For example, if you're tired or you have been feeling agitated or unwell, this might prevent your intuition from flowing.

5 Enjoy the process and take your time. You are building a relationship with the pendulum and your psychic mind. Like any kind of relationship, this can take time to establish but it is worth the effort.

Pendulum dowsing to purify a space

If you need to prepare a space for a psychic reading, you can use your pendulum to help find specific blockages or clusters of negative energy. Once identified, you can use the same pendulum to remove this energy.

You will need: Your pendulum and some space to walk around in the room you will perform your divination work.

1   Stand in the middle of the room and hold your pendulum. Center yourself by taking a few deep breaths.

2   Slowly walk around the room, asking "Is there any negative energy in this space that needs to be removed?" Take your time as you do this.

3   If the pendulum starts moving erratically, or with a "yes" response, then you know you're in the right spot.

4   Take a couple of long, deep breaths and, as you exhale, imagine you're breathing light and love into the space.

5   Now say out loud "Please remove this negative energy so that the space may be cleansed and filled with light." Stand still and wait for the pendulum to respond.

6   Once the energy has been removed, the pendulum will start to move in a positive manner. If there is no response, state your wish again.

7   Eventually, the pendulum will move to indicate that the space is purified and ready for divination work.

You can perform a similar purifying technique on yourself. Hold the pendulum above your head and ask it to identify any energy blockages as you move it steadily around the body. When the pendulum begins to swing, you'll know you've hit a cluster of negative energy that needs to be removed. Ask the pendulum to cleanse this part of your aura—which is the energy field that sits around your body (see pages 92–95)—then wait for it to respond.

CHAPTER TWO

SCRYING: CRYSTAL BALLS, MIRRORS, WATER, AND MORE

This chapter introduces you to scrying, which is the art of divining the future and gaining psychic insights and visions through a trancelike state, with the help of a tool to focus on.

An introduction to scrying

Scrying involves the use of a tool—which could be a pool of water, a crystal ball, a plain dark surface, or even the smoke from a flame—to provide a blank canvas on which the reader can cast their gaze. This promotes a meditative state whereupon the subconscious mind takes over and intuitive messages are received through imagery. The reader engages their senses, and the imagination, to build a picture that is reflected on the scrying tool. They then use their latent intuition to interpret the images they see. The images may come through in many different forms and it is up to you how you wish to decipher them, but to help you get started, turn to pages 135–137 for a list of the common symbols you might see, and their typical meanings.

Who does it work for?

Scrying works for everyone. The key is to remain open and engage the imagination. Children are particularly good at scrying for this reason. Unlike adults, children are not limited in their views or stifled by logic. They're prepared to believe in the unseen and appreciate the wonder of the world around them, which means it's easier for them to see and feel intuitively. A degree of patience and the ability to relax is needed for anyone wanting to turn their hand to scrying.

Early techniques

First recorded in ancient China around 3000 BCE and also in ancient Egypt in 2500 BCE, scrying was a favorite practice among the Ancients who were looking for ways to make sense of the world and to divine the future. The Ancients had a strong connection with the natural world, and this bond was an integral part of life and key to their survival. As such, Mother Nature became an entity and a friend, a goddess in her own right who could teach and guide. All they had to do was pay attention and seek out clues that might signify a change of fortune.

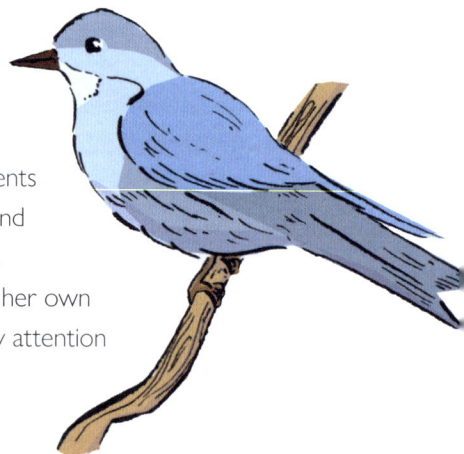

Our ancestors looked to the heavens for inspiration, deciphering the pattern of the stars and the changing shape of the Moon to ascertain when it was the best time to plant and sow, and when they could finally reap the rewards of their hard work with a plentiful harvest. They watched the birds migrating, and drew clues from this behavior, noting the direction of the wind and looking for other signs that might indicate a change in weather and circumstance. They saw signs everywhere, and while this might seem odd to us now, it was their way of making sense of the world, of predicting what was to come, and of tapping into the energy of the Earth.

A glimpse of sunlight on a rainy day may offer a chink of brightness in the modern world, but to the Ancients this was a portent of joy to come, a signal that all would be well—the rain would not last forever and good times were around the corner. From gazing into pools and ponds in search of patterns that might dictate destiny, to watching how swiftly the birds flew or reading the bones of an animal carcass, the tools may have differed from those used today, but the technique was the same. It relied on innate intuition, a little imagination, and the ability to connect with the natural world at a deeper level.

Some of the most popular forms of scrying, and how to make them work for you, are detailed on the following pages. Each practice differs slightly, utilizing a variety of tools and techniques. Find the one that appeals the most to you and have a go.

DID YOU KNOW?

Nostradamus was a sixteenth-century French seer and is one of the most notorious scryers in history, famously using a brass bowl—which was elevated on a stand and filled with liquid—to scry. His predictions, which are renowned around the world, were recorded in a book of poetic verses known as *Les Prophéties*.

Grounding ritual

Because scrying relies on your innate intuition, it's important to get into the correct mindset before you begin. In doing so, you'll be more open to receiving insights and you'll also be able to understand and interpret the signs and messages that you receive. Preparation is key, so take some time to clear your mind and relax with this simple breathing ritual.

You will need: Some space to sit in comfort, a white candle to promote feelings of peace, a match or lighter, and some amethyst, which is associated with psychic power.

1   To begin, light the candle and set your intention. For example, you could say "My intuition I ignite" or "I am open and ready to receive messages."

2   Get comfortable and sit with your back supported either by a wall or cushions and place the amethyst in front of you.

3   Roll your shoulders back to open your chest and your heart chakra (which is situated here and is connected with your emotions), then lengthen your spine.

4   Place your hands in your lap, palms facing upward and open as if ready to receive a gift. Take a couple of long, deep breaths while gazing at the candle flame, then close your eyes and visualize tree roots spreading from the soles of your feet, deep into the earth.

5   Take a long, slow breath in and feel it travel along the length of your spine, up through the back of your neck, and into the space behind your eyes. As you exhale, release the breath and imagine it continuing its journey upward, where it emerges through the center of your scalp.

6   Continue to breathe in this way for a couple of minutes until you feel completely relaxed.

7   Open your eyes and pick up the amethyst. Bring the stone close to the center of your forehead and hold it here.

8 Take a couple of deep breaths and imagine you are absorbing the radiant energy of this stone. See the energy as violet light, which bathes your head in a purple glow.

9 Say "I trust my intuition, all of the time. I am open and ready to receive a sign." Relax for a couple of minutes and focus on your breathing. You should now feel calm and ready to begin scrying.

Cloud gazing

An easy way to begin your scrying journey and get into the right mindset is to enjoy a spot of cloud gazing. This is something we often try as children, and it's a practice the Ancients used regularly to divine the future and receive guidance.

You will need: An outdoor space from which you can clearly see the sky, a blanket, your divination journal, and a pen.

1   On a warm, sunny day when there are lots of clouds in the sky, find a comfortable spot outside, such as a lush patch of grass, and lay your blanket down.

2   Lie down, relax, breathe deeply, and gaze up at the vista. What can you see? Enjoy the view—the beautiful blue of the sky and the soft, fluffy white clouds that glide overhead.

3   Now let your focus settle on a cloud, or a grouping of clouds, that catches your eye. What does it remind you of? Is there a clear picture forming?

4   As the cloud moves through the sky, it may elongate and transform before your eyes and this might trigger a narrative in your mind. Enjoy making up stories and deciphering the shapes you see.

5   Treat this as an imaginative game, and nothing more. There is no need to put pressure on yourself to see a specific "vision." This exercise is about stretching your imagination and stimulating your intuitive brain. Give yourself the time and freedom to be creative.

6   When you are ready, sit up, and record what you have seen in your journal.

TOP TIP

Cloud communication

As well as any images that might appear in the clouds, you could also consider other aspects of their appearance and movement.

- **Speed:** Fast-moving clouds could signify that an event or outcome will happen soon whereas clouds that are moving slowly might indicate longer-term changes.

- **Color and texture:** Soft, white clouds may suggest a period of happiness and positivity but if the clouds become dark and stormy, this could represent misfortune or difficult challenges ahead.

- **Size and shape:** A large, fluffy cloud may signal stability and security. A wispy or thin cloud could mean you have unfinished business or that something is uncertain.

Look to nature

Nature has the power to lift your spirits, soothe your soul, and help you find your place in the world. It allows you to see the bigger picture and can help to trigger the intuitive mind. Learning to connect with your surroundings and tap into the natural world will help to develop the psychic skills you need to perfect the art of scrying. There is nothing like finding your favorite spot in nature, taking a moment to find peace and gain perspective, and then looking for guidance.

You will need: Your divination journal, a pen, and a place in nature where you can sit without being disturbed.

1   Set yourself up in a comfortable position. Sit for a moment in stillness. Try not to move or let anything disturb your peace. Instead, concentrate on your breathing and the gentle rhythmic rise and fall of your chest.

2   Engage each of your senses in turn. First, notice what you can see. Let your gaze take in the view and nothing else. Hone your stare so that you focus on something within your viewpoint, such as a cluster of flowers that catch your eye in the distance. Notice everything about the flowers, from their size and shape to their color and the way they move in the breeze.

3   Next, consider what you can hear. What sounds greet you? Don't strain, just let the music of nature filter through. Does anything stand out? If so, try to pinpoint the strand of noise and which direction it is coming from.

4   Engage your sense of smell. Breathe deeply and notice how the air tastes and feels in your mouth. Is there a distinctive fragrance that springs to mind, perhaps the scent of freshly cut grass, or the smell of wild lavender?

5 Finally, consider what you can feel, from the breeze on your face to the sharp blades of grass under your hands.

6 Take a deep breath and ask for a sign, a message, or a prediction from nature. Do this silently or out loud. Let your body and mind relax and reach out with all of your senses. You might notice something that stands out to you—for example, the flowers you saw earlier may suddenly dance in a gust of wind, which makes you feel joyful and alive. This could be a sign that you need to take action on something. Perhaps you hear a sudden burst of birdsong, or the wind whips at your face and it's like a wake-up call. This might mean that something will happen out of the blue that will take you by surprise.

7 Record all of the things you notice. It doesn't matter how small they may seem. Write everything down because the meaning may become evident in the future. Reflect on your words and the things you have noticed and enjoy connecting with your environment in this intuitive way.

Crystal ball scrying

Best for: Those who struggle with meditation techniques and need a prompt or tool to help them relax.

What is it?

Crystal ball scrying, otherwise known as crystallomancy, is an ancient tradition that is commonly associated with traveling communities, notably the Romani people. The ball, which can be any type of crystal sphere, helps the reader drift into a meditative state by giving them something to focus on. The reader fixes their stare on the ball and lets any thoughts, images, or patterns materialize. For some readers, these will form in the mind, while for others they actually appear reflected on the surface of the ball. The act of crystal ball reading is more about helping the individual to focus their mind and tune into the higher self so that they can receive psychic insights.

Types of crystal ball

Some readers favor a clear glass ball, but it can be easier to scry with a dome of solid color—for example, an obsidian ball is dark and makes a good backdrop for images to form. A sphere made of rose quartz is made up of lots of chalky layers that naturally resemble shapes and patterns and this can help to trigger the imagination. The choice is down to the individual and the type of ball they feel drawn to.

It is worth getting a ball that is at least the size of your rolled up fist, so that you can see it clearly. Some readers like to hold the ball in both hands, while others prefer it to sit on a table untouched—again, this is down to personal preference and what feels best for you.

Crystal ball scrying step-by-step

1 Prepare your crystal ball by cleansing it in fresh water. Gently wipe the sphere clean using rainwater or water from a stream. If you don't have easy access to fresh water, use bottled water instead. You can also cleanse your crystal ball by leaving it on a sunny windowsill for a short period of time. The vibrant rays of light will remove any energetic residue left behind from previous readings. **Safety note:** Do not leave crystals in direct sunlight because this can pose a fire hazard.

2 Prepare yourself by sitting in stillness and taking some deep breaths to clear your mind. Make sure you are fully relaxed and open to receiving psychic messages. Create a soothing atmosphere by lighting candles and burning scented oil, such as lavender or geranium.

3 Connect with your crystal ball by holding it in both hands or by placing your hands gently on either side of the sphere. Let your gaze rest on the dome and continue to breathe deeply.

4 Hold your stare and try not to look away or let anything steal your attention. This can take some practice, but over time you will get used to focusing on the ball and nothing else. Soften your gaze and ask for a psychic message. Don't force this; just relax, breathe, and let any thoughts or images come naturally.

5 Engage your imagination. Go with what you see and feel. You may notice a pattern or narrative developing—let this unfold and see where it leads you.

6 Trust your subconscious mind to speak to you and deliver intuitive insights. Don't second-guess anything you see, simply take note of it for future reference.

Mirror scrying

Best for: Those who like the idea of working with magical tools and creating their own special mirror for the purpose of scrying.

What is it?

Scrying with a mirror is an ancient technique that is still hugely popular today. The reader gazes into the surface of the mirror, while going into a trancelike state to divine signs and psychic messages. Glass mirrors were first used for this purpose, but it's harder for the reader to tap into their intuition and glean imagery when faced with a clear reflection of themselves, so most people prefer to use black mirrors.

Types of mirror

A scrying mirror can be handheld or standalone. It is usually small to make it easy to maneuver and carry. The shape of the mirror does not matter. Some people use a regular glass mirror—while these are easy to obtain, they are usually only used by highly experienced readers. Black scrying mirrors are more common.

For black scrying mirrors, some people prefer to use mirrors that have been painted with black paint, which provides a dark, dense, nonreflective surface. This gives the reader a canvas to focus on without any distractions. These types of mirrors can be bought or you can easily make your own by painting the glass of a picture frame with black acrylic paint.

Other people like an onyx or obsidian mirror, which is crafted specifically for the purpose of scrying. While the hue is still black, this type of surface is layered and reflective, allowing light to dance on the surface and create shadows and shapes that can trigger the psychic senses. Obsidian (pictured right) is associated with protection and power; it helps to focus the mind, while also grounding the individual. The Aztecs were particularly fond of this crystal, using it in their own version of scrying and also in spiritual rituals.

Mirror scrying step-by-step

1 Set up your psychic space by creating the right atmosphere. You will need to be comfortable because you might be sitting for a lengthy period of time. You might want to dim any artificial light, close the curtains, light some candles, and set up some cushions and throws.

2 Prepare your mirror for the reading. Gently wipe it using lukewarm water while visualizing the mirror bathed in white light. If you haven't cleansed it recently, perform the cleansing ritual on pages 36–37.

3 Quieten your mind. Take a few deep breaths and focus on your intention. What do you want to know? Are you hoping to see a vision or a prediction for the future, or do you want an answer to a specific question?

4 Gaze into the surface of the mirror. Let your eyes soften and continue to breathe deeply. You might want to ask a question or simply let your mind wander and allow any thoughts or feelings arise. Don't strain or force your stare—instead, imagine you are winding down for the day and about to drift off into a daydream. In this state, you are more likely to receive messages from your subconscious mind, which is led by your intuition.

5 Record anything that you see or any thoughts or impressions that you have. Remember, psychic insights come in a number of forms so while you might not necessarily "see" anything at first, you might "feel" things or even receive an insight in the form of a narrative in your mind.

Cleanse your mirror

Caring for your mirror is as important as the mirror itself. It should be cleansed regularly to remove any type of negative psychic residue. There are a few ways you can do this. Some readers like to leave the mirror out beneath the light of the Moon—on a night when the Moon is waxing (getting bigger), or on the night of a full moon, when its power is most potent.

You can also bury the mirror in the earth, beneath a layer of soil. Leave the mirror overnight and retrieve it in the morning, then gently wipe away any dirt and debris. This practice allows any negative residue to be absorbed into the Earth.

Alternatively, try this simple smoke cleansing ritual, which can be carried out at any time.

You will need: Your scrying mirror, a bundle of dried sage leaves, a handful of dried lavender, a match, and a fireproof bowl.

1   Place the sage and the lavender in the bowl.

2   Strike the match and light the herbs. As you do this, say "By smoke and flames bright, cleanse this mirror for second sight."

3   Drop the match into the bowl and let the leaves burn.

4   Waft the scented smoke from the sage and lavender around your mirror, making sure it is completely engulfed in the sweet, smoky aroma.

When you have finished cleansing your mirror, wrap it in black silk or satin to protect it from picking up external energy, then store it somewhere safe. Retrieve the mirror when you are ready to use it and remember to cleanse it again after use.

Full moon water scrying

Best for: Those who are highly sensitive to emotions and feel a strong connection with the phases of the Moon.

What is it?

Full moon water scrying is a powerful form of divination that uses the light of the full moon to conjure images and predictions on the reflective surface of the water, which are then deciphered for their meaning. The water is a conduit for the Moon's mystical energy and the gentle light of the Moon brings illumination and insight.

The use of the Moon as a tool for divination is nothing new. This orb has been harnessed in magical rituals for centuries and its shifting shape has long been a source of fascination around the world. The Moon is at the pinnacle of its power when in its fullest form, which is why it is best to perform water scrying under a full moon.

Types of full moon water scrying

Some people prefer to get out into nature and find a stream or river that they can sit by. This allows time to reflect and connect with the environment while also harnessing the power of a full moon. If you feel a strong affinity with the natural world, this type of full moon water scrying would be ideal.

For others, it is easier to take a bowl of fresh water outside and sit beneath the light of the Moon. An alternative would be to leave a bowl of water outside beneath the light of the full moon, retrieve it in the morning, and then gaze into the water to glean any insights. While this is the easiest and quickest type of moon water scrying, it is not as powerful as sitting beneath the light of the Moon on the night of a full moon, when psychic energy is thought to be at its most prominent.

Full moon water scrying step-by-step

1   You may wish to practice with a bowl of water before moving on to scrying with natural bodies of water. If possible, choose a dark-colored bowl because it's easier to see any reflections and images on a darker background. Half-fill the bowl with fresh water and add a couple of drops of lavender essential oil to promote the flow of psychic energy.

2   Wait until the full moon is visible in the sky. You need to choose a location where you can sit beneath the light of the Moon. Once you've found your ideal spot, get comfortable because you could be here for a while. Take blankets and cushions and wrap up warm if it's a cold night.

3   Sit holding the bowl in both hands. Try to relax as you do this by taking several long, deep breaths. With each breath, imagine that your psychic chakra—which is positioned in the center of your forehead and known as the "third eye"—is gradually opening. If it helps, visualize an eye in this location, opening fully.

4   Ask the Moon for a message or vision, then turn your attention to the surface of the water. Watch the reflections of light swirling within and let your imagination take over. You might see shapes, patterns, and images emerging, or even a narrative. Let the visions unfold and simply be aware of them.

5   Relax. If nothing happens, that's okay. You can always try again. The evenings either side of the full moon are filled with psychic energy, so you can repeat the process the next day.

Smoke scrying

Best for: Those who enjoy performing practical rituals and who can be impatient when it comes to seeing results.

What is it?

Also known as capnomancy, smoke scrying is the art of reading and deciphering images within the smoke from any type of fire. Usually, it's an intentional practice and the fire or flame is set for a purpose, but it can be done at any time and provides almost instant results. Popular with shamans around the world, smoke scrying is a quick way of tapping into your intuition to receive answers and insights, and can be done at any stage when the fire or flame is lit.

Types of smoke scrying

Smoke scrying can be performed on a smaller scale with candles and incense, or it can be carried out around a larger campfire. Candles and incense are used for personal messages. The way the smoke travels and the shape it produces can trigger psychic insights. In particular, tealights are a quick way to ask a "yes" or "no" question. The reader lights the tealight, focuses their mind, asks the question, then snuffs out the candle. If there is a lot of smoke, this is seen as a positive "yes" answer, while little smoke means the answer is "no."

A larger campfire can be used for more in-depth predictions. The reader looks at the point where the flames meet the smoke for images and patterns to decipher. The shapes they see often form part of a narrative, which can be used to predict the future. For example, you might see what looks like a horse—a symbol of movement and action—followed by the shape of a house, which might indicate you will be moving home.

Smoke scrying step-by-step

1   Set your intention and what you would like to know, because this will dictate your choice of tools. For example, if it's a personal insight or a reading for a friend, you might choose a full candle, but if you want a quick response, pick a tealight.

2   Light the fire or candle and watch as the flame develops. Use this time to still your mind by focusing on the light of the flame(s). Breathe deeply and ask for a message or prediction.

3   Notice the smoke. Is there a lot of it? Which direction is it going in? If it seems to lean toward you, that might suggest something important to you, but if it leans away, the prediction could be for someone else.

4   Soften your gaze and engage your imagination. What shapes do you see in the smoke? What do they mean? Trust your instincts and let any thoughts arise.

5   Ask a specific question before you snuff the candle out and notice how much smoke is generated. An abundance of smoke indicates success while a little smoke suggests that things may not go in your favor.

TOP TIP
Candle colors

If you are using candles, your choice of color is significant. White candles can be used for all general readings, but you can tailor your scrying to a specific area by choosing the right hue. For example, red is associated with passion, movement, and action so it's a good choice if the querent wants to focus on achieving a goal. The same principle applies when choosing colored inks for ink scrying (see page 42).

Red: Passion, love, movement, and action.

Pink: Love and romance.

Green: Money and prosperity.

Gold/Yellow: Success and fame.

Blue: Health and well-being.

Black: Protection, power, and strength.

Brown: Family and home.

Purple: Spirituality, intuition, dreams, and career matters.

Ink scrying

Best for: Complete beginners and those who want to flex their scrying muscles.

What is it?

Ink scrying is a fairly recent invention that uses the combination of water in a bowl and different colored inks to enhance psychic visions. A small bowl is half-filled with clear water, then a vial of ink is added. In some cases, the reader may add a few drops to start with and build up the amount they use. They may also need to mix the ink in the water by swirling the bowl in their hands. The images and pictures created by the ink form the basis of the reading.

Types of ink scrying

While you can buy ink that has been specially crafted for scrying purposes (for example, it might have been infused with specific herbs to enhance its magical power), any type of ink can be used. Scrying inks are usually dark in color, such as black or navy blue, because darker colors show up well in the water, making it easier for the reader to see the shapes formed by the ink. However, any color of ink can be used and, just as with candles, you can tailor the ink color to your question or aim (see the top tip box on page 41). Any type of water can be used, but reading from water that has been left out under a full moon will add the Moon's energy to the process.

Ink scrying step-by-step

1 Get your tools ready. Half-fill your bowl with water and have the ink that you're going to use to hand. Set everything out before you, so that you can spend a few minutes in quiet contemplation before you begin your reading.

2 Calm your mind by focusing on your breathing. Count to four slowly as you inhale and repeat as you exhale. Once you've got into a rhythm with this, extend the breath by an extra count. If your mind wanders, bring it back by focusing on your breath.

3 Add the ink to the water carefully, then take the bowl in both hands and swirl the water gently. As you do this, consider what you'd like to know—what questions do you have? Take a minute to close your eyes as the water settles.

4 Gaze into the bowl and look at the patterns and images created. What do you see? If you're struggling, give the bowl a swirl and take another look. Let thoughts float into your mind and acknowledge them.

5 Record your findings in your divination journal so that you can reflect on them at a later date. Readings often become clear once you've had some time to consider each image fully and meditate on it.

SCRYING TIPS

This chapter has outlined some of the most popular scrying techniques, but this is in no way a complete list. Scrying can be done anytime, anywhere, and with almost any tool. As long as you have time, space, and a plain surface that you can focus on, you have all you need to get started. You simply need to rely on your ability to get into a meditative state and to engage your imagination. For some, scrying is an easy way to predict the future, but even if you're not a natural, with a little practice you'll soon find your latent psychic skills developing. To help you on your scrying journey, consider the following tips and tricks.

Be patient

Scrying takes practice and patience. You might not see results during your first few attempts but it's worth sticking with it. You will notice a change over time as you become more adept at connecting with your intuition and engaging your imagination. To help with this, make a record of each scrying attempt in your journal. This will help you pinpoint your predictions as and when they happen. You will be able to reflect on your scrying and see the progress you are making.

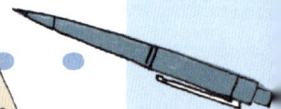

Breathe

Deep breathing is a great way to focus the mind and clear the head. If you're struggling with any of the scrying techniques outlined, take a couple of long, deep breaths, then try again. You could also try listening to a guided breathing meditation before you begin a scrying session, perhaps on a breathing app on your phone.

Follow your heart

It seems obvious, but scrying is a unique experience and each individual will have a different way of doing it. Over time, you will discover what works for you, and what doesn't. Trust your intuition and go with what feels right. Create your own rituals; for example, you could perform a cleansing practice (such as the one on page 52) before you begin or find that going for a walk helps to clear your head in preparation for a scrying session. For some, playing background music helps, while others prefer complete silence and stillness to get into the zone. Consider the atmosphere you wish to create and set the scene for yourself—you might want to burn scented oil or incense, light candles, and say a few affirmations. Alternatively, you might prefer to scry with minimal fuss, going with the flow of your day and doing it when you feel in the right frame of mind. The approach you take is entirely up to you.

Focus on your third eye chakra

The third eye chakra, which is associated with the flow of psychic energy and your intuition, is located in the middle of the forehead. When this energy center is triggered, you become open to intuitive insights. If you're having problems scrying, it might be because this chakra is blocked, or not fully open.

To help with this, spend some time focusing on your third eye chakra in quiet meditation. Hold a piece of amethyst (see page 28), which is associated with psychic energy, over your third eye and visualize a purple flower bud. With every exhalation, imagine the petals of the flower unfurling, until the bloom is fully open. Alternatively, perform the third eye ritual on page 131.

Research different techniques

If scrying interests you and you enjoy the techniques outlined in this chapter, take it a step further and research other scrying methods. The Ancients were huge fans of scrying and had many methods of predicting the future, which are still used today. You could look to different mythologies and spiritual schools for inspiration. A quick search on the internet should set you off on the right path if you want to delve further, or you could check out some books on the subject.

CHAPTER THREE

CLEROMANCY: RUNES, STICKS, CHARMS, AND DICE

In this chapter, you will learn about cleromancy, which is the collective name for a group of divination techniques that involve casting sticks, stones, and other materials on the ground for psychic insight.

An introduction to cleromancy

To perform cleromancy, the reader chooses a selection of materials that can be cast down onto a surface. These materials are crafted into fortune-telling tools, with each item being assigned a specific meaning. The reader uses either the meaning of each object facing upward, or the pattern created by the way their tools fall, to make a prediction. For example, stones are usually marked with symbols that carry certain meanings, or, if casting dice, the number sequence is interpreted. Sometimes, objects like stones or charms are drawn from a casting bag or box, in the case of runes (see pages 54–61), for example. The querent can ask a question and pull out a number of rune stones to use for the reading.

Who does it work for?

Cleromancy is something anyone can do. There's an element of game playing to this psychic practice—whether you're rolling dice or scattering sticks, the results occur by chance and rely on the reader's ability to decipher the meaning, using a combination of skill, psychic ability, and imagination.

If you enjoy studying and learning and like to be organized, then cleromancy will appeal to you because, for the most part, you'll be working with preexisting systems that have meaning. It can take time to get to grips with your tool, but persistence pays off and you'll improve your knowledge of ancient practices and mythologies in the process.

Early systems

Originating from the Greek word *kleros*, meaning "lot" or "inheritance," cleromancy in its earliest form was a process used to determine a person's "lot" in life and to make a number of key life and death decisions. Casting lots is an ancient form of ritual that has been around since the dawn of time and provides the basis for most types of cleromancy. The Greek gods were thought to enjoy this practice, with one early narrative suggesting the brothers Zeus, Poseidon, and Hades cast lots to determine who would govern the different realms of the earthly plane.

Animal bones—usually ankle bones because of their minute size—were typically used for casting lots, but early humans were inventive and used a number of other materials, including animal entrails, human knucklebones, shells, and pebbles, to divine the future. While tossing stones and bones was the obvious and easiest choice at the time, the ancient Romans formalized things by cutting strips of wood from nut-bearing trees, adorning each one with a symbol, and casting the twigs onto a white cloth. From this, they could not only predict future outcomes but also make major battle decisions.

The Norse people adopted their own alphabetical system, known as runes, to cast lots and for divination. Each stone was carved with a specific marking, which held symbolic meaning and could be interpreted in a number of ways. Further east, in countries like Nepal, futures were revealed on the roll of a dice, while people in Japan drew sacred lots using paper with written predictions (see page 53), a practice which is still popular in some parts of the country today.

Some of the most common and popular types of cleromancy used today are described in this chapter. Most of these have ancient origins, but there are modern alternatives that you can try. Enjoy experimenting and finding the system that works for you.

Cleansing ritual

Cleromancy is an art form that relies on specific casting tools. The reader develops a personal, psychic connection with their tool of choice. To do this effectively, the reader must first cleanse themselves and also purify the space in which they're going to work.

You will need: A bowl of hot water and a bundle of fresh sage and rosemary.

1   Add the fresh herbs to the bowl of steaming water. You might want to mix this carefully using a spoon.

2   Sit with the bowl in front of you and take a long, deep breath in through your nose. Inhale the fresh scent and let it reach the back of your throat.

3   Hold the breath in the center of your chest and imagine that the astringent aroma is traveling through your body, clearing away any negative energy.

4   Release the breath slowly through your mouth. As you do this, visualize a stream of black residue filtering from your lips. This is the negative energy and tension that you have been holding on to finally leaving your body.

5   Repeat this process at least three more times, picturing the breath sweeping through you to clear any blockages.

6   Place the bowl in the area where you are going to conduct the reading and, using your hand, waft the scented steam around the space. You might want to carry the bowl around the room as you do this. Say "I cleanse and purify this space with light and love."

7   Leave the bowl in a safe position as the water cools.

Paper predictions

While it's tempting to start with an ancient form of casting, more modern practices also work, and can help you flex your psychic muscles while developing your confidence. Take inspiration from the Japanese tradition of paper casting.

You will need: A few sheets of plain paper, a notebook, a pen, and a bowl.

1 Cut or tear the paper up into small, similar sized squares that can easily be folded. Each piece should look roughly the same so that you can't distinguish between them.

2 Think of your predictions—take your time and have fun with this. Here are some ideas: "Good fortune will smile on you," "Love is around the corner," "Expect success for your hard work," and "Take your time when making decisions." Include some more challenging predictions, too. For example, "A sudden obstacle prevents you from making headway."

3 Make a list of your predictions in the notebook so that you can see if any are too similar, then slowly tick them off as you write each one on a square piece of paper.

4 Fold all of the pieces of paper up, place them into the bowl, and give it a gentle shake. Depending on the time you have, draw a small handful and cast them down on a flat surface, or if you prefer, pull one out of the bowl. Read the prediction(s) and ponder on the meaning(s). Even if it doesn't make sense now, make a note of it so that you can refer back and see if it comes true.

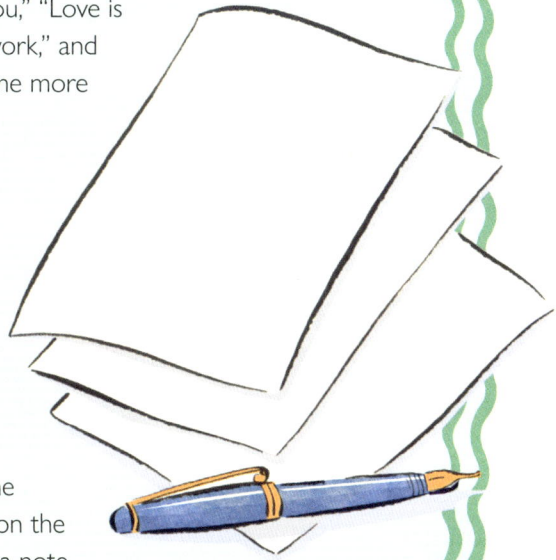

Some people prefer to select a daily or weekly prediction. If you plan to carry on using the paper predictions, you might want to place them in a sealed jar and position this on your nightstand so that you can draw one each morning. Alternatively, pop the jar by your front door and pick one as you leave your home every day.

Reading runes

Best for: Those with an interest in Norse mythology and spirituality, and for anyone who likes to explore the significance of symbols.

What is it?

The runes are a Germanic alphabetical system. There are a few variations of the runic alphabet, including the Elder Futhark and the Younger Futhark. Originally used by early Norse people in written form, these mystical symbols, which are mostly linear in shape, were often carved into boats for safe travel and into shields and weaponry for protection and strength. They were also used to mark graves and in magical rituals to petition the gods.

Each rune has a distinct energy that can be harnessed to heal and manifest. According to legend, the runes were given to the father god Odin (pictured on page 54) after he spent nine days and nights hanging from the World Tree, known as Yggdrasil. As a reward for this sacrifice, he was given the knowledge of the runes, which he then passed on to his people so that they could communicate effectively and also connect with the spiritual realm.

The runic symbols are often carved into individual wooden pieces or inscribed on a set of stones. Runes are usually small and roundish in shape, making them easy to carry in a charm bag. They can be picked singularly to answer a question or cast down onto a flat surface. The runes that fall face up are the ones that provide the reading. Some people like to pick three runes to represent the past, the present, and the future, and then decipher the meaning of each one.

Types of runes

The Elder Futhark runic alphabet was used from the second century CE onward, and includes 24 symbols with a range of mystical meanings (see pages 56–59). The Kylver Stone, which was found in a tomb in Gotland, Sweden, is a fifth-century limestone slab inscribed with a selection of these runes. This early representation shows the importance of the Elder Futhark and demonstrates its use to not only mark and protect graves, but also to bind the soul of the dead person within.

The Younger Futhark alphabet, which was devised later, around the eighth to ninth century, is a much-simplified version of the original Futhark. Often called the Scandinavian runes, this set has only 16 symbols. The Elder Futhark, being the first form of the alphabet, is the one that is most commonly used for divination purposes.

Runes were traditionally carved into wood or stone but more modern interpretations may be crafted from polished crystals, such as quartz, amethyst, and obsidian. The choice of material is entirely up to the reader. While crystals have a distinct energy that can enhance a reading (see page 16), stones and wooden runes are connected to the Earth and are more similar to the original runes that were used by those early Norse seers.

Rune meanings

Each of the 24 runes that make up the Elder Futhark runic alphabet carries deep meaning—here is a brief summary of key themes each one represents. If you are considering using the runes in your divinatory practice, it's worth immersing yourself in the deeper meanings and interpretations, and studying Norse spirituality, so that you are fully versed in this form of divination. It's also worth bearing in mind that the names of the runes can vary slightly between sources so you may see them listed elsewhere with alternative spellings.

Fehu: Related to cattle and livestock, Fehu is a symbol of wealth, abundance, fertility, and stability within the home.

Uruz: This rune represents the wild ox. It is associated with strength, tenacity, life force, and courage, and suggests progression in any area of life.

Thurisaz: Also known as the thorn, this rune embodies the giants, who were the enemies of the Norse gods. As such, it signifies brutal force, unexpected change, and conflict.

Ansuz: Symbolizing the mouth, Ansuz indicates communication, knowledge, and inspiration and is often linked to the Norse god, Odin.

Raido: This rune represents a wagon and is related to movement and travel. It is synonymous with spontaneity.

Kennaz: The rune of fire, Kennaz signifies a torch and is a symbol of a creative spark. It is associated with inspiration and vision.

Gebo: The gift rune, Gebo is often linked to partnership and balance. It can represent a spiritual gift or talent, and also generosity between two people.

Wunjo: Synonymous with joy, this positive rune embodies all aspects of emotional fulfillment, success, and harmony.

Hagalaz: Representing hail, Hagalaz can be disruptive in influence. It is associated with delays and troubles and it symbolizes the ability to overcome obstacles.

Nauthiz: This is the rune of need. Related to restriction and endurance, it signifies challenges and situations from which we can learn and move forward.

Isa: Like the ice that this rune represents, Isa is synonymous with clarity and focus. It suggests a time of introspection and watching and waiting to see how things progress.

Jera: Associated with the cycles of life, this is the rune of the harvest, of reaping rewards, and of reaching goals.

Eihwaz: A symbol of the yew tree and linked to the World Tree in Norse mythology, Eihwaz signifies enlightenment and the balance between life and death.

Perthro: Synonymous with life's mysteries, this rune relates to fate, destiny, and occult knowledge. It can also signify a time when secrets are revealed.

Algiz: The rune of the elk, Algiz is linked to protection and guardianship. It hints at inner wisdom and trusting intuition.

Sowilo: Representing the Sun to the Norse people, this rune is associated with vitality, good health, and victory. It represents balance and wholeness.

Tiwaz: Symbolizing the Norse god of justice, Tyr, this rune relates to strength, leadership, and the ability to come to an agreement.

Berkana: This rune signifies the birch tree, linking it to regeneration and healing. It embodies feminine energy and is often connected with fertility.

Ehwaz: Associated with the horse, Ehwaz represents physical movement or a shift in circumstance. It is synonymous with progression and success.

Mannaz: A symbol of humankind, Mannaz relates to community, cooperation, and friendship. It is the rune of teamwork and coming together to create something positive.

Laguz: The rune of water, Laguz indicates intuition and the emotions. It is connected with dreams, hopes, and fears, and is a sign to go with the flow.

Inguz: Known as the seed, this rune embodies growth, achievement, and personal development. It is associated with the hearth and home.

Othala: The rune of inheritance, Othala represents the ancestors and the gifts, both physical and spiritual, that have been passed down.

Dagaz: A symbol of the dawn, this rune is synonymous with new beginnings and often suggests some form of awakening and a sense of enlightenment.

Reading runes step-by-step

1   Quietly meditate with your runes before giving a reading. This will help you connect with their power. Sit with your rune bag in your hands, close your eyes, and take some deep breaths. Imagine drawing the energy of the runes in with each inhalation. As you exhale, release any tension or stress. This will put you in the right mindset for a reading.

2   Decide which type of reading would work best for you. If you're looking for an answer to a question, then draw one rune from the bag and consider the meaning. If you want a general reading, which provides insight and helps you move forward, draw three runes from the bag to represent the past, the present, and the future. For those wanting to connect with the runes on a deeper level, gather a handful of runes and cast them down—look at the way they fall, the shape they create, and the runes that face upward to decipher the meaning.

3   Be intuitive in your interpretations. While each rune has a specific energy and meaning, it's also worth considering your initial response to the rune and the reading as a whole. Don't restrict yourself by focusing solely on the runes' original meanings. Rune readings have many layers; they can be taken literally or interpreted in a spiritual way, with the focus being on the querent's life path and true purpose. If you are working with more than one rune, consider the implications that each rune has on the others and build a picture based on this.

4   Practice deciphering the runes. This ancient form of prediction can be complex and it may take many attempts before you're fluent in your interpretations. If you enjoy studying, and you like to take your time before coming to conclusions, then this is definitely the divination tool for you.

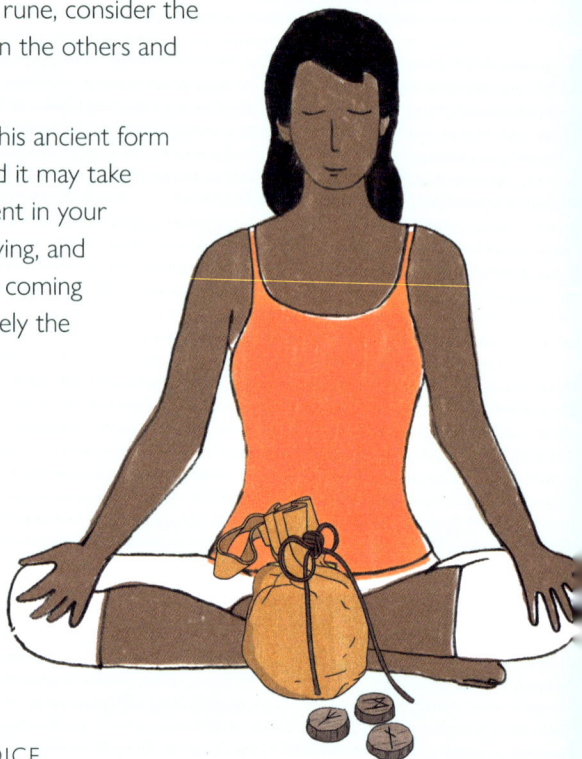

Make your own runes

While there are plenty of stores that sell sets of runes, the process of making your own is both enjoyable and beneficial. It allows you to fully connect with each rune that you craft. The good news is, you don't have to be particularly skilled to make your own. Some people like to carve wooden runes, but this relies on a certain amount of woodworking skill. If you're a complete beginner, it's easier to make them from stones, and the beauty of this is that you can head into nature and enjoy foraging for them.

You will need: A set of 24 stones of roughly the same size, a permanent marker pen, a small fabric bag or pouch, some paper, and a regular pen.

1   Clean the stones to remove any debris, then set them out in front of you in a line.

2   Practice drawing each rune marking on paper to make sure you know exactly what you're doing. Refer to pages 56–59 for the symbols of the Elder Futhark runes.

3   Next, consider each rune in turn and what it means, then pick a stone from your selection that calls to you and draw the rune on its surface.

4   Take your time with this process. There is no rush and you can think about the meaning and energy of each rune as you work.

5   When you have a complete set, make sure the ink is dry and pop them carefully in the bag you set aside.

6   To charge and cleanse your runes, you can place a crystal inside the bag. Clear quartz helps to magnify the energy of the stones, while also purifying them. Amethyst is also a popular choice because it heightens psychic power.

NOTE

Always check local laws before collecting natural materials and do not take anything from privately owned land without permission.

Throwing the sticks

Best for: Those who love foraging in woodland and enjoy using their imagination.

What is it?

Throwing the sticks is an ancient type of divination adopted by many different spiritualities throughout Europe and North America. It involves casting a handful of similar sized sticks, which are kept solely for the purpose of prediction, onto the ground. The reader then looks at the pattern created by the sticks to divine the future. It's a shamanic practice, allowing the practitioner to connect with nature and the landscape, and use their psychic skills to interpret the meaning. While the Ancients favored stones for this type of cleromancy, sticks were easily accessible, portable, and lightweight. They were often stored in a special animal skin bag, which the reader wore on their person.

Types of stick

Sticks come in all shapes and sizes. You can use any form of stick for this divination method, but you might choose to fashion your sticks using wood from a specific type of tree. The Celts, who favored this type of divination, believed that different types of trees had unique energies that could be harnessed in magical rituals, and so sticks were often made from a specific wood for this reason. Consult the guide to some popular trees and their meanings on the opposite page, then refer to page 64 for instructions on how to make your own set of sticks.

Tree guide

Ash: Connected to magic and healing.

Beech: Synonymous with knowledge and feminine power.

Birch: Linked to renewal, purification, and fertility.

Hawthorn: A fairy favorite, associated with sorcery and creativity.

Hazel: Connected to wisdom, inspiration, and magic.

Oak: Synonymous with strength and protection.

Sycamore: Linked to sacred power and divinity.

Willow: Associated with the Moon, psychic energy, and prediction.

Throwing the sticks step-by-step

1 Prepare a clean, flat surface where you can cast your sticks. A table or work top is fine, but you might prefer a patch of grass. While this is slightly more uneven, it enhances the natural power of the sticks. If you're inside, you might want to light some candles to create the right atmosphere.

2 Still your mind by taking some deep breaths. Close your eyes and sit in silence for a few minutes. Allow thoughts to come and go but try not to hold on to them. When you feel suitably relaxed, you are ready to set your intention.

3 Focus on the type of reading you would like to perform. Do you want a specific answer to a question, or to concentrate on an area of life, or are you looking for a general sign about the future? Have your purpose clear because this will help you when it comes to decoding the sticks.

4 Close your eyes, reach into your stick bag or box, and pull out a bundle of sticks. Hold them in both hands. Focus on your intention and then gently throw the sticks down onto your chosen surface.

5 Open your eyes and open your mind. Gaze at the pattern created by the sticks and let your imagination take over. What can you see? Is there a specific image coming through, or perhaps a pattern or letter? Let your mind wander and allow any thoughts or feelings to arise.

6 Record anything that you see or feel in your divination journal. An image might not make sense at first, but over time and on reflection, you might understand the meaning, so it's important to keep a log of each reading you do.

Make your own sticks

To help you connect with the natural energy of the sticks, it's a great idea to gather and fashion your own. In doing so, you create a bond with your divination tool, which will help you when casting and deciphering a reading. It's relatively easy to make your own set. If you're looking for a specific type of wood, do some research first to establish which kind of trees are in abundance.

You will need: Access to some woodland, a rucksack, a sharp knife or strong pair of scissors, some sandpaper, and a special bag, pouch, or wooden box.

1   Find some woodland or a small coppice and go for a stroll. Relax as you walk and engage all of your senses. Breathe deeply and ask Mother Nature to guide you in finding the right type of sticks for the purpose of divination.

2   Look at the base of trees for any fallen sticks or twigs. Start collecting them and placing them in your rucksack as you go. Opt for twigs that you are drawn to, letting your heart take the lead on this. You could take a couple of larger sticks that you can cut down, or you could go for smaller, broken bits of wood; it's entirely up to you. You will need between 12 and 20 sticks in total.

3   Once you have an ample supply of wood, find a comfortable spot to sit beneath the boughs of a tree.

4   Use the knife or scissors to carefully cut the sticks. They should all be roughly the same size and they will need to be small enough to hold in your hands before casting.

5   Gently smooth the bark of the sticks with the sandpaper. You don't have to go for a smooth finish if you prefer the sticks in their natural state, but make sure they are easy and safe to handle, so get rid of any sharp knobbly bits that might cut your hands.

6   When you have finished, lay the sticks around you and take a moment to connect with them. You could say a few words or a magical affirmation, such as "I connect with the energy of nature; my psychic senses work with the sacred power of the sticks to divine the future."

7   To finish, pick up each stick and place it in your stick bag or box, then give thanks to nature for this special gift.

TOP TIP

Alternative tools

If you don't want to throw sticks, there are plenty of other tools you can cast in exactly the same way, if the intention and energy is correct.

Coins can be given specific meanings. For example, a large gold coin could signify the gift of abundance, while a smaller gold coin could mean a slight improvement in fortune. A silver coin could be related to success, while a copper coin might indicate love, because copper is associated with Venus, the Roman goddess of love. Keys are also a great alternative and can be thrown down for an immediate answer. If the key points upward, this indicates a "yes" response; if the key points downward, this means the answer is "no."

Some people like to collect and throw feathers because they are renowned for their spiritual energy. While feathers can be more troublesome to handle, particularly if you choose to do a reading outside, they come in a range of sizes and hues, which can help when it comes to deciphering predictions. Don't be afraid to experiment when practicing the art of cleromancy and use the tools that are available to you.

Charm casting

Best for: Those who like to collect interesting objects and who need something to stimulate their imagination.

What is it?

Charm casting is a modern form of cleromancy that has become extremely popular. The reader has a selection of different charms, which are usually small items that they have collected for this purpose, such as trinkets, beads, and items of jewelry. These are usually kept in a charm bag or box. The reader dips their hand inside and grabs a handful of charms to cast on a plain, flat surface. In some cases, the surface is segregated into sections, which relate to different areas of the querent's life, such as "love," "family," "health," and "wealth." The reader makes a note of where certain charms have fallen, and does a mini reading based on this and what each charm means. They form a picture in their mind, which is created by the arrangement of charms on the table and what each individual item represents.

Types of charm

Charms used for this type of prediction vary but are usually of a similar size. Fancy buttons, unusual gemstones, shells, jewelry, beads, and other trinkets or lucky charms may be used. Each charm is attributed a specific meaning. For example, a shell, being from the sea, might be related to travel over water or linked to the emotions, while a coin would be linked to finances and a positive sign that wealth is on the way.

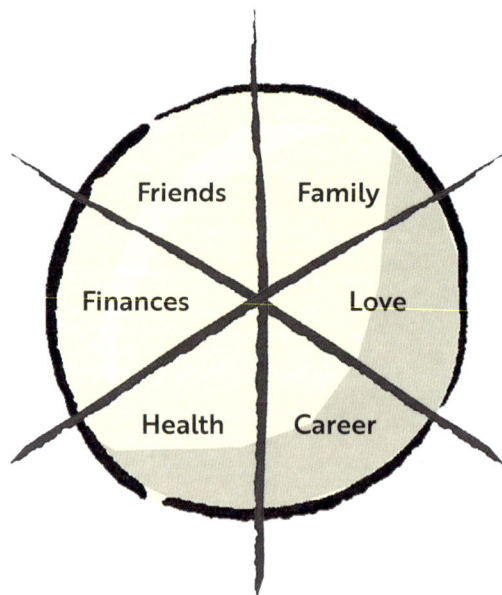

Charm casting step-by-step

1 Gather your charms together. You will need a large selection to provide variety and trigger your imagination. It's important to know what each charm means to you. Spend time with each item, holding it in your hands and connecting with its energy. Breathe deeply, relax, and let any thoughts or feelings come to mind.

2 Cleanse your charms. Place the charms in a black satin or velvet scarf, along with a piece of quartz crystal, which will cleanse and amplify their energy. Tie up the bundle and leave overnight.

3 Create your board or flat surface. Depending on your preference, this could be a flat surface like a table, that you keep solely for the purpose of scrying, a sheet of plain card, or a piece of wood. You might want to create separate sections on the board that represent different areas of life. This can be done by marking these out or just by using your imagination.

4 Clear your mind before you begin casting. Focus on any specific questions or areas that you need help with. Close your eyes and dip your hand into the bag or box. Let your fingers rifle through the charms and then grab a handful and cast them on to your board.

5 Breathe, relax, and let your imagination take over. What do you see? Is there a pattern? Which charms stand out, and where have they fallen? Can you see a picture developing? Build a narrative in your head and enjoy being creative with your interpretation.

Dice divination

Best for: Those who like playing dice games and adding up numbers. This technique also works for those who seek an immediate answer to a question.

What is it?

This ancient form of divination falls under the category of astragalomancy, which comes from the Greek word *astragalos*, meaning "dice" or "knucklebone." Indeed, many early civilizations, such as the Sumerians who lived over 5,000 years ago, used sheep's knucklebones in the practice of casting, looking at the shapes and the way the bones fell to divine the future.

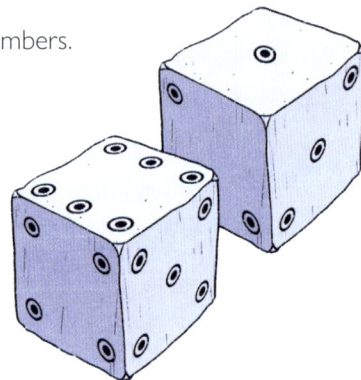

Dice have existed in one form or another for thousands of years, with the earliest representations of the six-sided version found in ancient Egypt. Dice reading was also popular in ancient China and reference of the practice has been discovered in sacred manuscripts dating from the Han Dynasty, which ran from the second century BCE to the second century CE.

Astragalomancy is still hugely popular today as a form of prediction. It involves the throwing of a number of dice to divine an answer or prediction. Practitioners may throw the dice once or several times to create a series of numbers, which have a preordained meaning (see pages 70–71).

Types of dice divination

The method of throwing the dice varies depending on the type of reading you would like. A singular die can be used for "yes" and "no" answers to a question, with odd numbers meaning "no" and even numbers meaning "yes." Any type of dice may be used, but cubes are usually favored, with markings or numbers from one through six.

If you're looking for something more in depth, then you might want to double up on your die or even use three, rolling them at the same time. It's common for dice readers to create a circle within which to cast the dice. This can help when forming pictures based on the way the dice fall. Any that fall outside of the lines are usually considered void and disregarded.

Dice divination step-by-step

1 Decide how many dice you're going to use. Beginners might find it easier to start with one. Some readers like to have a dice cup, which can be as simple as an egg cup or another small vessel, from which they cast the dice, but if you're using your hands then spend a few minutes holding the die or dice and connecting with their energy.

2 Breathe deeply to clear your mind. Consider what you would like to know. If you have a straightforward question, ask it, either out loud or in your head. If you want to conduct a more general reading, then simply clear your head and ask for a prediction.

3 Close your eyes and roll the die or dice onto a flat surface. Do this in one sweeping movement, and if you're using a defined circle, be sure you don't roll the dice too hard. Otherwise, they might fall over the lines.

4 Trust your intuition. While each number has a specific meaning (see pages 70–71), you might find that you get a flash of inspiration or an intuitive insight to go with this. Be open and go with how you feel. If you think the answer or reading is unclear, then roll the dice again until you feel you have clarity.

DID YOU KNOW?

Dice divination was favored along the Silk Road, where stones or bones were carved into elongated rectangles and marked with the numbers one through four. These dice were thrown three times, with the resulting trigrams (the line patterns formed by the number sequences) recorded and referenced in a divination manual to predict the future.

Dice numbers and combinations

Here are potential meanings for numbers one through eighteen. This includes every possible combination when using between one and three six-sided dice.

One: The number one indicates the ego and a sense of self-importance. This roll can suggest some sort of strife or troublesome situation surfacing.

Two: Indicating duplicity and not being aware of the full picture, this number reminds us that there are two sides to every story and situation. It can also relate to couples and relationships.

Three: A fortunate omen, the number three signifies a positive outcome and new beginnings. It's synonymous with good luck and celebration.

Four: This number suggests a setback or delay. The querent may find it hard to progress in any area at this time.

Five: Whether it is news from afar or a visit from an old friend, the number five signifies something new that will bring much joy.

Six: Considered an unlucky roll, this number can relate to an ending of sorts and a time of turmoil for the querent.

Seven: An unsettling life phase, the number seven indicates a time when everything is up in the air and things are erratic.

Eight: This is a roll that signals taking time out to see things from every perspective. It often suggests a period of slow progress.

Nine: A lucky number that relates to love and passion, nine can suggest a new relationship or the rekindling of existing love and strengthening family ties.

Ten: This roll is auspicious and indicates a period of success. Creativity is flowing, and there's an abundance of good fortune.

Eleven: This number suggests there may be an illness or other obstacle that is slowing things down. This is only temporary; change is on the way.

Twelve: The number twelve signals great news that could be related to business, finance, or legal issues. There is recognition and reward for past efforts.

Thirteen: This roll can suggest a stressful period and going within to find answers. Things may not go to plan but there is a light at the end of the tunnel.

Fourteen: Community and social gatherings will be well starred if this number is rolled. Family celebrations may also occur.

Fifteen: This is a roll that signifies a change in friendships or relationships, which can be positive or negative.

Sixteen: This number indicates travel and adventure ahead. The querent will be broadening their horizons and may venture further afield.

Seventeen: This roll signals an emotional time when feelings may change. This number urges the querent to be open and compassionate and to go with the flow.

Eighteen: An extremely lucky roll, this number suggests great success; a victory is highlighted and goals will be attained.

CLEROMANCY TIPS

This chapter has detailed some of the most popular forms of cleromancy. These methods rely on specific tools, some of which were used by ancient civilizations as a form of communication and to divine the future. Each method has its merits. Casting using items that have personal meaning is a potent way to predict the future and gain insight, but like any form of divination, it takes time and practice to perfect. Here are a few simple tips and suggestions to help you make progress.

Study your method

Whether you've chosen the Norse runes, or you prefer to get to grips with rolling dice, the key to success is to know your chosen method inside out. Study each form by reading up on its history. Learn the myths and legends associated with your chosen type of casting and familiarize yourself with different ways of doing it. Get to know the meaning of each stone or number sequence. While you might not use every bit of information that you glean, the knowledge you gain will help to build confidence.

Form a personal relationship

Don't wait until the moment you want to do a reading to handle your sticks, stones, charms, or dice. Get used to the feel of them beforehand. Sit with your casting tools in stillness and connect with their energies. Meditate on each one, and familiarize yourself with their size and shape.

Stretch your imagination

As with many forms of prediction, cleromancy works better if you can engage your imagination, so while you may know the meaning of certain stones, charms, or number combinations, don't let this dictate the reading. Relax and let your subconscious take over. If you get an impression or feeling, use that in your final interpretation and let a story unfold.

Find your own path

Each type of casting tool is distinctive in the way it is used, but don't let that limit you. If you feel drawn to using a different technique, go with it. Develop your own reading methods and make them personal to you. Cleromancy is a practice that relies on habit and procedure, so take the time to devise your own way of doing things and trust your instincts.

CHAPTER FOUR

READING THE BODY: HANDS, FEET, and AURAS

This chapter explores the practice of body reading, which involves either looking at a person as a whole, or studying a particular part of their body, to divine their fate.

An introduction to reading the body

Each individual is unique, so it makes sense that their physical makeup could reveal facts about their personality, traits, and gifts, and also their approach to life. In particular, body parts such as the hands, face, and feet can be examined in detail to ascertain insights and foretell a person's future.

This makes a lot of sense if you consider body reading in its simplest form—the Ancients would have looked at a person's hands and feet and noted any rough or calloused skin. From this, they might have surmised that the person was a practical, hard worker, most likely exposed to the elements on a daily basis. The reader formed a conclusion, which they then took further with a prediction that this person might live a happy, simple life and be blessed with good health.

Who does it work for?

If you're looking for an easy to way to assess a person and get a general overview of who they are and what makes them tick, then body reading is the practice for you. Quick insights can be gained at first glance, but if you wish to dig deeper then you'll need to study each body part in detail—for example, learn about the structure of the hand, its lines, and mounts and what they can tell you (see pages 79–87). If you enjoy one-to-one contact with others and like social interaction then this could be the best form of divination for you.

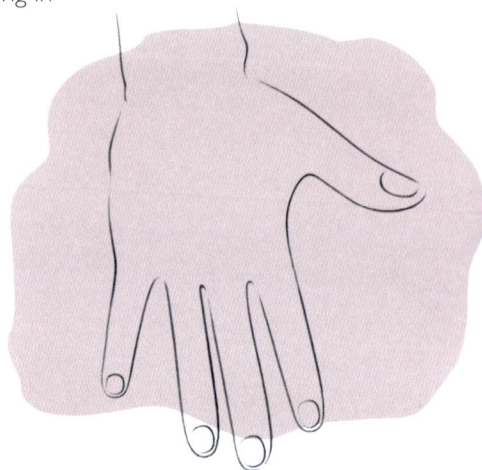

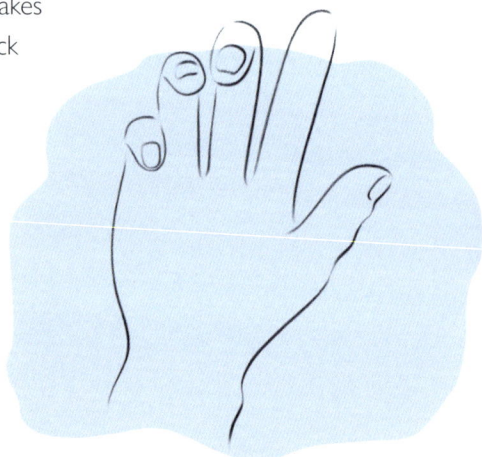

Early techniques

Although it's difficult to pinpoint the exact origins of body reading, the practice finds its roots in ancient India, where it was used to divine a person's destiny. Known as Samudrika Shastra in Sanskrit, face and body reading, and also palm reading, which was included under this moniker, were highly revered practices. The distinctive lines and fingerprints on the hand, which are unique to each individual, were thought to reveal the future fate and type of life an individual might lead.

From India, palm reading spread to China and then to Persia, Egypt, and Greece, where it was championed by the philosopher and scientist Aristotle, who wrote about it in great detail. During the Middle Ages, palmistry took a back seat, mainly because of the church's influence and distaste for divination, but by the Renaissance, there was renewed interest, and during the nineteenth century, palm reading experienced a full-on revival, with various books and papers compiled on the subject.

This chapter discusses some of the most popular forms of body reading—palm reading, foot reading, and aura reading—which are still in use today. The ability to tell the future and make a prediction by looking at a part of the body is a mix of common sense, psychic skill, and knowledge, based on ancient practices. Have fun experimenting with this type of divination and practicing on yourself and your nearest and dearest.

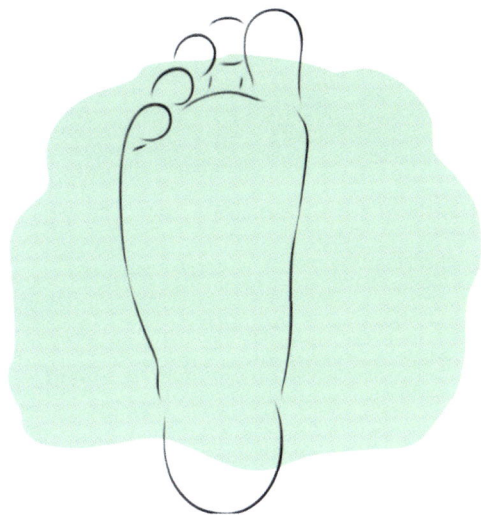

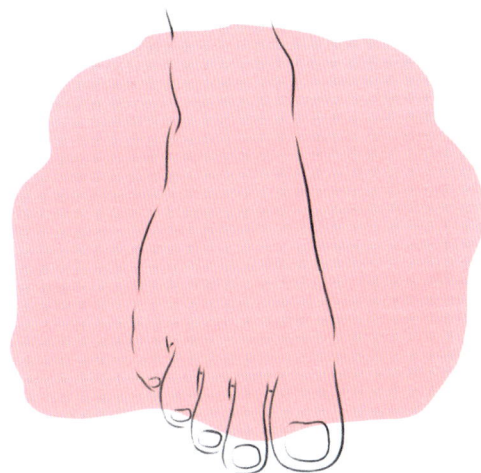

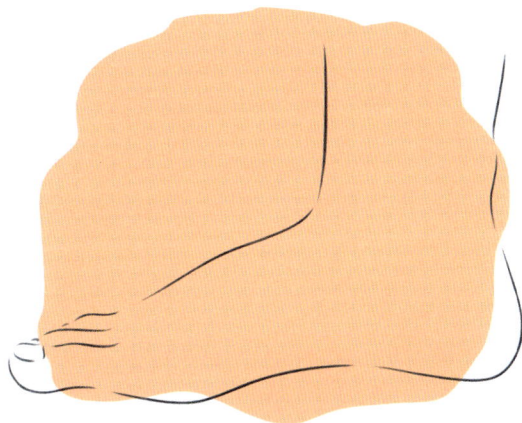

Breathing ritual

A calm and relaxed body and mind is key for these types of readings. You will be tuning into another person, so you need to clear your thoughts so that they don't interfere with the communication. One of the best ways to do this is through breathwork. Set yourself ten minutes before you start body reading to perform this simple breathing ritual, which stills the mind and helps to release tension from the body.

You will need: Some space to stand and stretch.

1   Stand with your feet hip-width apart and roll your shoulders back. Lengthen your spine and imagine a thread traveling up your spine and emerging through the top of your head. Feel the thread gently tugging you upward, so that you stand straight and tall.

2   Take a long, deep breath in and imagine you're drawing the air through the soles of your feet, up along your legs and your spine, and into your lungs. As you do this, place both palms over your heart in the center of your chest.

3   Hold the breath for the count of four long beats then release the breath slowly through pursed lips, letting your hands drop by your sides. Feel your chest expand as you do so.

4   Breathe in again, inhaling deeply, and place your palms over your heart. This time, hold the breath for five long beats. As you exhale and drop your hands to your sides, imagine that you're releasing any tension or stress from your body and mind.

5   Continue to breathe in this way for a few minutes, or until you feel more relaxed.

6   If any thoughts come into your head, try not to hold on to them. Instead, release them with each out-breath.

7   When you've finished, give your body a gentle shake. You might want to perform a few simple stretches—you could reach upward with both hands in a star shape and then sweep your arms and hands down to the floor.

Palmistry

Best for: Those who like the challenge of learning something new and looking at finite details.

What is it?

Palmistry, also known as chiromancy, is the art of palm reading. The reader studies the size, shape, and markings of the palm to decipher the querent's personality traits and to predict their future. The idea is that the lines on the palms change over time to reveal a person's fate, so readings provide a current picture of how things look but may change depending on personal circumstances. Popular in ancient Rome, it is thought that this type of prediction originated in India, and soon spread throughout Europe, being a prominent fortune-telling practice in Romani culture.

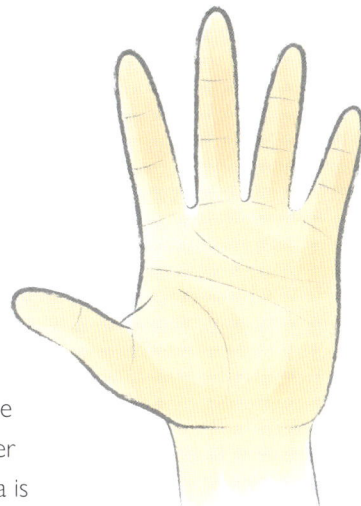

Types of palm readings

There are typically four main lines on the palm—the head line, the heart line, the life line, and the fate line (see pages 81–84)—that are studied when performing a reading, along with the mounts, which are the fleshy areas at the base of the thumb and fingers, and at the bottom of the palm (see pages 85–87). The reader will also take other things into consideration, such as the length of the fingers. For example, long, slender fingers could denote a creative, sensitive soul, whereas short, fatter fingers suggest someone who is logical and easygoing. Other factors, such as the size and shape of the palm, are also taken into account—square-shaped palms represent practicality, while longer, slender palms hint at a dreamer with a vivid imagination.

The querent's skin texture and general appearance of the palm may also be studied. A fleshy palm denotes someone who wears their heart on their sleeve and takes an enthusiastic approach to life, while a thin, bony hand indicates that the person is more reserved and cautious. Some readers will only look at the dominant hand, while others like to study both hands, believing that the left denotes the past and the right indicates future events.

Palmistry step-by-step

1 Breathe and clear your mind before you begin. Take a moment to center yourself. Roll your shoulders back and lengthen your spine. Draw a breath in and imagine that as you exhale you are clearing away any obstructions to your psychic ability.

2 Decide which hand you will work with, or if you are going to use both hands for the reading.

3 Stretch the palm wide so that the lines are clearly defined and you have a full view of the hand. If you're reading for someone else, take their hand gently, palm upward, and hold the palm open so that you can study it.

4 Broaden your perspective. Hand reading is not simply about the lines and what you see on the palm. Be prepared to take in the general size, shape, and feel of each hand, and also any first impressions you have when looking at someone's palm.

5 Identify the four main lines (see pages 81–84) and the mounts (see pages 85–87) and get a general impression of their strength, size, and depth, then let any thoughts or observations rise to the surface of your mind. If you're reading for yourself, you might want to make a note of your findings so that you can refer back to them. If you're reading for someone else, simply let your intuition take over and allow your impressions to flow.

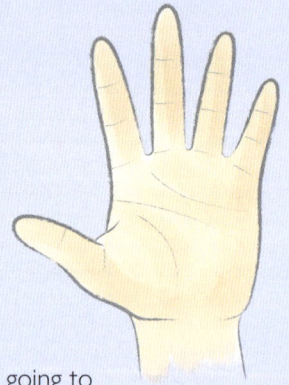

The lines of the palm

The head line

Starting under the knuckle of the index finger, the head line slices across the middle of the palm, spreading to the other side. Sometimes, it may dwindle down toward the wrist. This line, also known as the line of wisdom, relates to the intellect and how the individual thinks.

If the head line is clearly defined, then this is a person who is blessed with clarity, a focused individual who knows what they want. A weak head line suggests someone who is easily confused and has a lot going on in their mind. They may be full of ideas and slightly eccentric in their approach to life.

Sometimes, the head line will be short, and this can indicate someone who is spontaneous, and who makes swift decisions on the spur of the moment. A straight head line suggests someone who is levelheaded and logical, while a curved one shows a person who goes with the flow and likes to think outside the box. Often, the head line will change over time as the person becomes more self-assured.

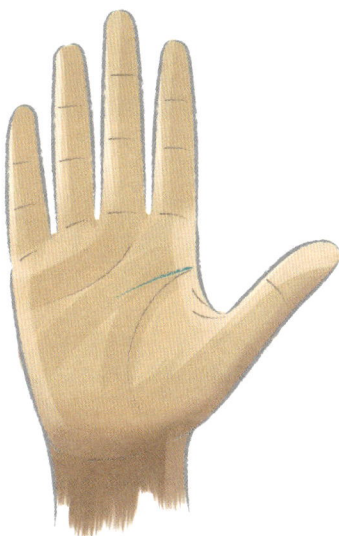

Short head line

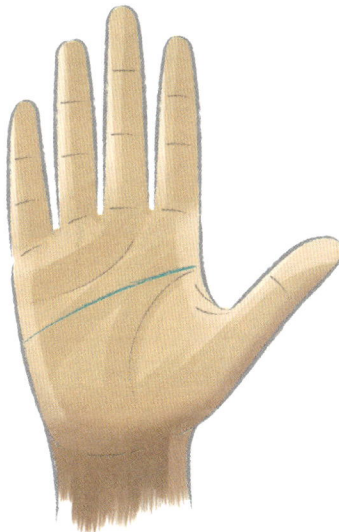

Long, straight head line

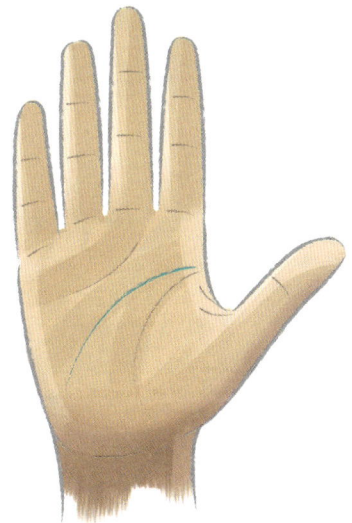

Long, curved head line

The heart line

Extending from beneath the knuckle of the little finger and sweeping upward to finish somewhere near or between the index finger and the middle finger, this line dictates your love life and how you handle emotions.

A short heart line indicates a lack of interest in relationships, or a brief love affair, while a long, deeply ingrained line suggests the querent is or will be content romantically—this is a person who seeks and needs love in their life. Should the line be broken or crossed with shorter lines, then it's likely this person has suffered emotional trauma or loss, while a loop within the line indicates sadness.

A prominent, curved heart line suggests that the person is openhearted and happy expressing how they feel, while a fainter heart line indicates that they feel uncomfortable with any type of emotion. A straight heart line shows someone who is logical and practical when it comes to affairs of the heart. If the heart line touches the life line, it's likely the individual may get their heart broken a few times during their life.

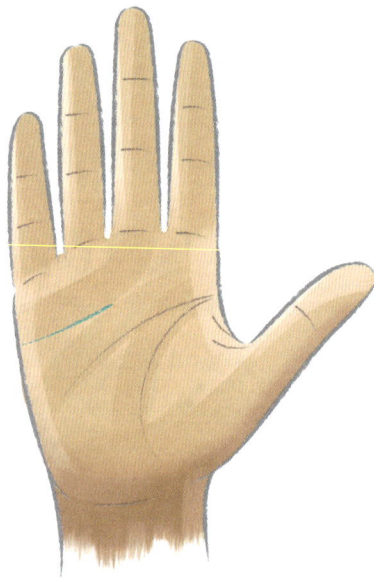

Short heart line

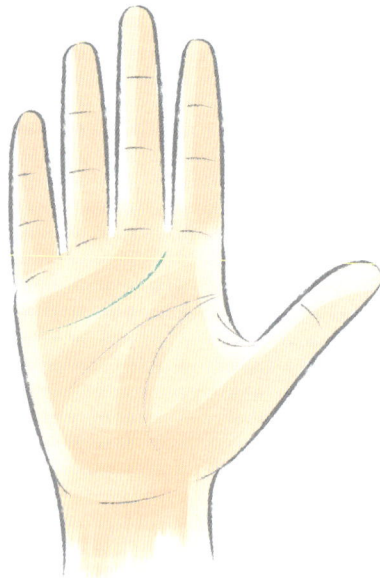

Long, curved heart line

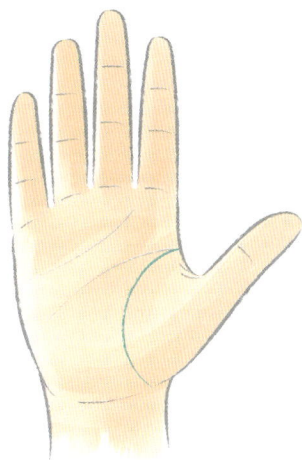

Long, curved life line

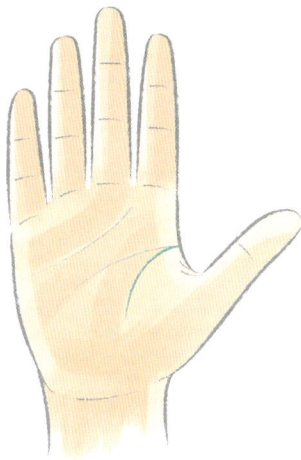

Short life line

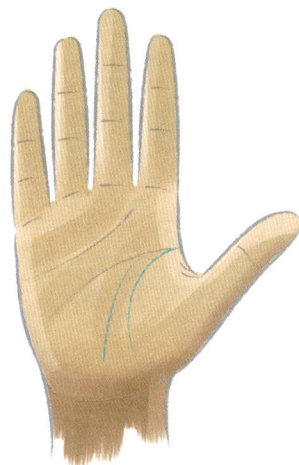

Double life line

The life line

Many people assume the life line reveals the length of a person's time on Earth, but in truth it's related to the general health and well-being of the individual and reflects major and minor events that might change their fortune. This line denotes energy and balance because it begins at the root of the thumb near the mount of Venus (see page 85), which is associated with vitality.

If the arc of the line is a strong curve, it's likely the querent has lots of energy and potential. This is a person who is enthusiastic and wants to make their mark in the world. A shorter arc suggests a person who can be listless and needs motivation at times. If the line starts quite close to the base of the thumb it's likely that the person feels tired a lot of the time.

The depth of the life line reveals an individual's drive, and the likelihood of success. If the line is deeply ingrained, it's likely that they will go on to create or make something of themselves. If the line is faint, they might be easily manipulated by others and lacking in direction.

Some people have a number of life lines close together, which shows lots of energy and many changes ahead. A break in the life line indicates that there will be a change in attitude or direction at some point in the future.

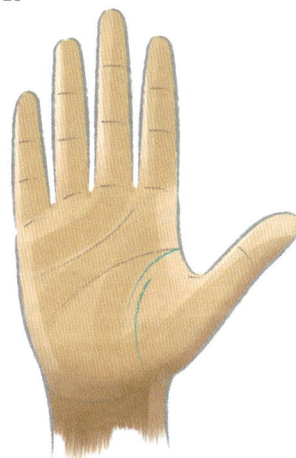

Broken life line

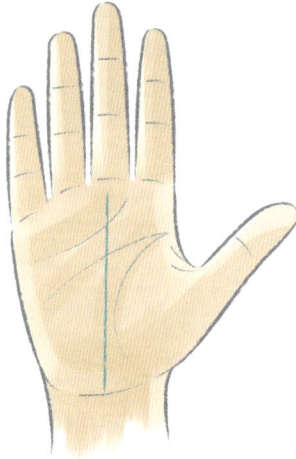

Long, straight fate line   Cracked fate line   Broken fate line

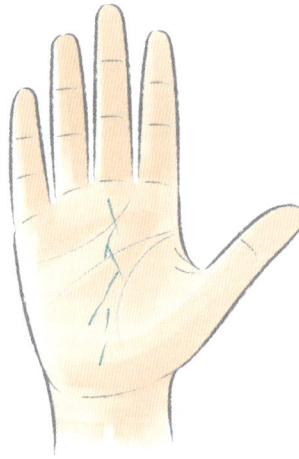

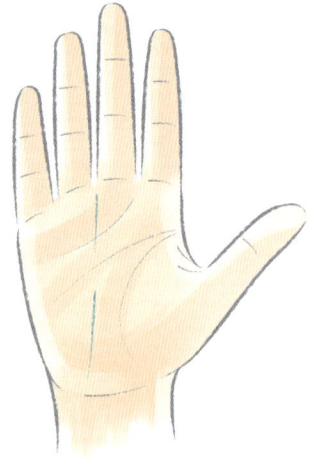

The fate line

Also known as the line of destiny, the fate line begins near the base of the wrist and travels upward to the fingers. It's a good indicator of the general success of the individual and reveals the effects of external circumstances and changes in fate.

If the line is long and strong, then it's likely that the individual will find their true life's purpose and feel fulfilled. A deeply ingrained line suggests that fate plays a key role in their success. If the line has lots of bends and cracks, this suggests the person will change direction many times, and a clear break shows that they might uproot in some way or transform their life completely.

A fate line that joins up with a head line early on suggests that this person knows what they want and probably had a clear ambition from a young age—this is often seen in self-made individuals or leaders. A fate line that joins the life line midway through suggests support from family and friends, and that choices made will be influenced by others.

The mounts of the palm

The mounts are the fleshy areas found under each finger, and toward the base of the palm. Named after the classical planets, the mounts reveal a person's passions and interests and can indicate their ideal career. Assess how big the mounts are for a full picture of an individual's destiny. Here we are working with six of the mounts that are easiest to identify; the mounts of Mars have been omitted.

- Jupiter
- Saturn
- Apollo/Sun
- Mercury
- Venus
- Luna/Moon

MOUNT OF JUPITER

- **Position:** Underneath the index finger.

- **Relates to:** Self-confidence and esteem, innate wisdom, and the ability to judge a situation.

- **If it is raised:** This person is confident and self-assured; a natural and powerful leader imbued with wisdom.

- **If it is flat:** This person suffers with their self-esteem and may lack confidence.

- **Look out for:** An inflated mount, which suggests the person can be arrogant and aggressive at times.

MOUNT OF SATURN

- **Position:** Underneath the middle finger.

- **Relates to:** Discipline and a person's attitude to work and life in general.

- **If it is raised:** This person is responsible and organized; they can apply themselves to any task and they strive to lead a balanced life.

- **If it is flat:** This person is disorganized and struggles to prioritize; they may also appear superficial to others.

- **Look out for:** An overdeveloped mount, which could mean that the person has bouts of depression.

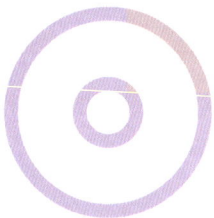

MOUNT OF APOLLO/SUN

- **Position:** Underneath the ring finger.

- **Relates to:** Creativity and imagination; it reveals how passionate and enthusiastic an individual is.

- **If it is raised:** This person is creative and knows how to express themselves. They're likely to be ambitious and driven to succeed.

- **If it is flat:** This person lacks aspiration and imagination. They have little interest in power or status.

- **Look out for:** A huge mount, which suggests vanity and extravagance. It's likely that this person is self-absorbed.

MOUNT OF MERCURY

- **Position:** Below the little finger.

- **Relates to:** The acquisition of wealth and information; it reveals if an individual is intuitive and resourceful.

- **If it is raised:** This person is highly intuitive and quick-witted. They will be proactive and able to create abundance throughout their life.

- **If it is flat:** This person is shy and withdrawn at times. They may need steering in the right direction.

- **Look out for:** An overdeveloped mount, which suggests a willful individual who is driven by greed.

MOUNT OF VENUS

- **Position:** Underneath the thumb at the base of the palm.

- **Relates to:** Affairs of the heart, romance, and pleasure.

- **If it is raised:** This person is highly empathic and values the relationships in their life. Likely to be motivated by love, they have an open heart.

- **If it is flat:** This person prefers a solitary existence. While they may have a couple of close friends or relations, they don't need love to thrive.

- **Look out for:** An extremely big mount, which suggests overindulgence and an addictive personality.

MOUNT OF LUNA/MOON

- **Position:** Underneath the little finger at the base of the palm.

- **Relates to:** The emotional world of the individual and how sensitive they are when dealing with others. Also linked to the intuition and the subconscious mind.

- **If it is raised:** This person is an emotional individual who tends to feel and sense things. They are also likely to have vivid dreams.

- **If it is flat:** This person struggles to show how they feel and can be closed off at times.

- **Look out for:** A highly developed mount, which indicates a person who lives in a fantasy world. It's likely this person struggles with everyday life and responsibility.

Solestry

Best for: Those fascinated by feet who fancy trying a fun and different type of prediction, which focuses mainly on personality traits and gifts.

What is it?

Also called solestry, foot reading has been practiced for thousands of years in India and China. Unlike reflexology—which focuses on a person's state of health and uses parts of the foot to correspond with specific body parts—solestry concentrates on the personality, and highlights the person's special gifts and qualities while also covering areas like family, relationships, and outside influences that may affect the individual in the future. The emotional state of the person and their general mood can be assessed when looking at the foot and taking into account its appearance, size, and texture.

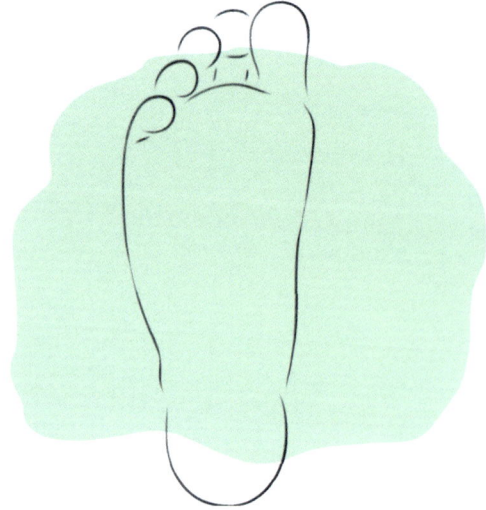

Types of foot readings

While there are certain things you can look for when practicing the art of solestry, it's up to the individual reader how they wish to proceed. Some readers like to consider both feet and believe that the left foot reveals the past and the right foot shows future events and influences. Some readers only use one foot and focus on every aspect from skin tone and texture to size, shape, and length of the toes. In general, the upper side of the foot relates to the image projected to the outside world, while the sole represents the internal and emotional world of the individual. Turn to pages 90–91 for some tips on what the size and shape of a person's foot and toes could reveal.

Solestry step-by-step

1 Familiarize yourself with the structure of the foot and what each part reveals. Study images before you begin and work with your own feet first so that you have a good idea of what to look out for.

2 Observe the foot from every angle. If you're reading for someone else, don't be tempted to touch the foot. Instead, vary your perception by looking from each side and from a distance. Also be sure to study the sole and to look at the top of the foot. Get an overall picture of it in your mind, then let your natural intuition take over.

3 Make notes of what you see, especially if you're starting out reading for others. This will help you to build a complete picture, which you can refer back to as you give your reading.

4 Explain what you see to the querent. For example, if they have high arches, discuss what this means in terms of traits and qualities and ask if they can relate to this. If you're reading for yourself, be honest about your gifts and flaws and consider if it matches your personality.

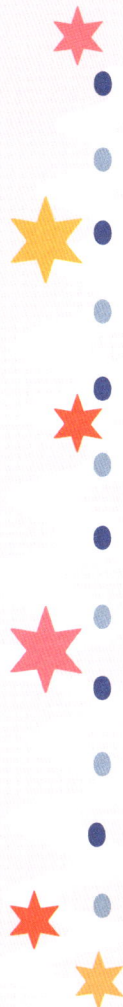

Foot size and shape

Assessing the size and shape of the foot will provide a general overview of someone's personality traits.

- **Wide feet:** These tend to belong to someone who is practical and reliable. They denote a person who isn't afraid to put the work in to achieve what they want.

- **Narrow feet:** This is a person who enjoys the luxuries of life. They have an eye for design and like to be surrounded by beautiful things.

- **Long feet:** The Chinese might refer to long, slender feet as "princess feet," the thought being that anyone sporting these delicate appendages was born to be waited on and can, at times, be self-indulgent.

- **Low arches:** Also known as being flat-footed, if you have low arches, you are likely to be sociable and friendly. You enjoy the company of others and have extrovert tendencies.

- **High arches:** Someone with high arches is likely to be independent and not afraid to stand out from the crowd. This attribute can suggest someone who is rigid in their viewpoint.

- **Graduating toes:** If each toe is slightly longer than the one before, and the toes graduate in a neat line, then it's likely that the person is methodical and thorough in their attitude to life and work. This is someone who applies themselves wholeheartedly to every task and is a perfectionist.

Toe telling

The toes are the most revealing part of a foot reading. They give an insight into your personality and the way you approach life. Here's a quick guide on what to look for and what each toe can reveal.

Big toe

If your big toe is on the small side, then it's likely you're good at delegating and you know how to get what you want using your innate charm. If your big toe is large, this is a sign of creativity and intelligence; you are inventive and buzzing with ideas, but you may struggle to implement them.

Second toe

If you have a long second toe, then you're an independent soul and a natural born leader. You make your own way in life and can be willful at times. It's said that in ancient India, mothers would warn their sons not to marry a girl with a long second toe for this reason! A shorter second toe denotes a person who is happy to take their time and doesn't need to always be in control. Those with a second toe longer than their big toe (a condition known as Morton's Toe) are thought to be highly energetic and adventurous.

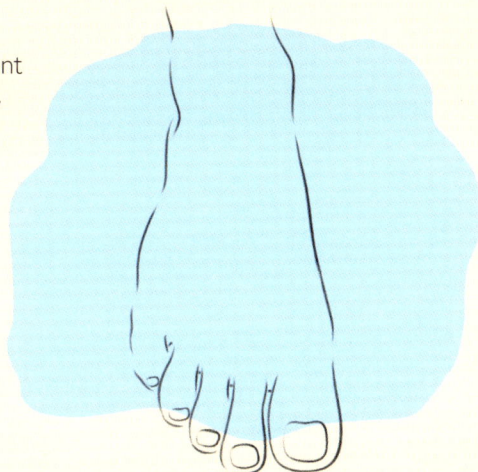

Third toe

In Chinese folklore and astrology, the third toe is associated with drive and ambition. Those with a long third toe aspire to greatness and will do all they can to succeed in their chosen career. These hardworking souls are perfectionists, and will always do their best, sometimes to the detriment of their own health. Those with a much smaller third toe have an easygoing approach to life and work. They don't like to be rushed and prefer to enjoy themselves.

Fourth toe

If the fourth toe is curled, it's likely you are a sensitive person who takes on other people's problems. Your nurturing side makes you a good listener. If the fourth toe is long and straight, family is important to you, and you care deeply about the welfare of others, while a shorter fourth toe shows that you keep your distance from loved ones and prefer your own company, relationships aren't as important to you, and you're probably more focused on business and career matters.

Little toe

A tiny little toe reveals a playful side to your personality. You're likely to be youthful in appearance and attitude and you love to have fun. A regular-sized little toe reveals a person with a responsible nature—this is someone who sticks to the rules and likes order and routine. If your little toe curls to the side, with the nail facing out rather than up, then you're a rebel at heart; you have an unconventional attitude and like to do things your own way!

Aura reading

Best for: Those who think visually and have developed their psychic skills to the point where they feel confident giving readings of all types.

What is it?

An aura reading is done by gazing at the shape and color of a person's aura, which is the electromagnetic force field that surrounds the body. The reader will go into a meditative trance, enabling them to see this invisible force field. This gives the reader a sense of the querent's state of mind, general health, and current issues by looking at the colors and the brightness of the aura. Some readers like to sketch the aura to help them tune into the person. Others use their intuition and tap into the aura by being in the querent's physical presence to offer insights and guidance.

Types of aura

Everyone has an aura but they vary greatly in color and shape, depending on the person's mood and state of health. A generally healthy and relaxed person will have a fairly bright, white aura. If they're having a bad time, their aura will be filled with shadows and dark gray to black splodges, which represent blockages and stagnant energy. See page 94 for the meanings of other colored auras.

The position of each color, or shadow, reveals even more. For example, if there is a dark cloud surrounding the querent's head, this might indicate depression and negative thoughts, or simply that they are suffering with anxiety and indecision, whereas a sunny yellow or golden glow might show they are feeling positive and full of joy. If the color is farther away from the person, this indicates future circumstances.

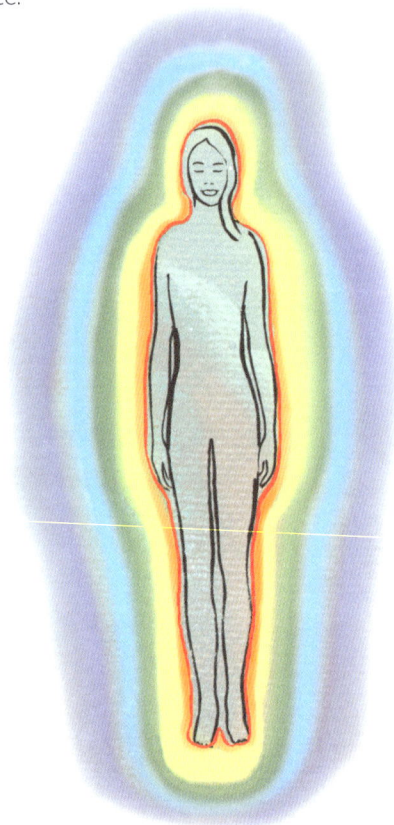

Aura reading step-by-step

1 Set up a mirror in front of a blank-colored wall, so that you can read your aura to start with. Position yourself in front of the mirror, and make sure you are comfortable—you might want to sit on a chair.

2 Draw in a long, deep breath and, as you exhale, imagine your consciousness is expanding outside of your body. To help visualize your aura getting bolder and brighter, see it as a thick halo that encircles you. Continue to breathe in this way and slowly bring your attention to your reflection.

3 Focus on the middle of your forehead and gaze at this spot in the mirror. Let your eyes soften and gently expand your attention outward from this point, so that you are taking in the outline of your head in your peripheral vision. You might begin to notice a shimmering energy or even see darts of color emerging. Try to stay calm and let the picture emerge steadily.

4 Expand your awareness even further and take in your entire reflection. Remember to keep your gaze relaxed and to breathe deeply as you do this. Don't worry if you can't see anything at first; aura reading takes a lot of patience and practice.

5 Once you become adept at reading your own aura, you can move on to reading for others. Try the practice on page 13 to help you tune in to the other person's energy before you begin.

Aura colors

To help you interpret your aura readings, here are some of the colors you might see and their corresponding meanings.

- **Red:** Action, movement, and passion. A red aura can indicate that the person is feeling passionate and determined.

- **Orange:** Vitality and creativity. An orange aura usually relates to joyful feelings, enthusiasm, and good health.

- **Yellow:** Fun, optimism, and self-esteem. A yellow aura indicates an open mind and new adventures, and that the querent is feeling confident.

- **Green:** Fertility, growth, and warmth. Synonymous with nature, a green aura shows a nurturing energy and indicates openness.

- **Blue:** Compassion, integrity, and self-expression. Associated with healing, a blue aura might suggest that the querent is recovering or helping someone recover from illness or upset.

- **Pink:** Love, romance, and kindness. A pink aura often indicates a new relationship or that the querent is feeling loved up.

- **Purple:** Psychic awareness and spirituality. If there is a lot of purple in the aura, the querent is highly intuitive and may have an interest in the esoteric.

- **Violet:** Inventiveness and the higher self. A violet aura shows that the querent is a gifted medium or psychic. This person is on a journey to find their true life's purpose.

- **White:** Peace, purity, and balance. A white aura indicates that the querent is feeling centered and well.

- **Black/Brown:** Negative energy and stress. Clumps of both shades indicate dark, pessimistic thoughts and that the querent may be holding on to guilt or anger.

- **Gray:** Stagnant energy and indecision. Often associated with worry and exhaustion, shades of gray in the aura suggest the querent is feeling under the weather.

- **Rainbow:** If an aura is awash with rainbow shades, then it's likely the querent is spiritually advanced, fulfilled, and feeling enlightened. This is the color of spiritual leaders and healers.

Crystal colors

There are many ways to perfect your aura-reading skills, but practice is the most important. While you might struggle to read other people's auras at first, any living thing has an energy force field that you can potentially "see." All you need is an object to focus on and some time to develop your gifts. Crystals make ideal aura-reading subjects because they have a very specific energy that emanates from within. You can position them anywhere, they don't move, and they're also portable, meaning you can practice at any time.

You will need: A place to sit in comfort and a crystal—any type will do, but quartz, citrine, and amethyst (pictured left to right above) are known for their powerful energies.

1 Place the crystal at eye height so that it is easy to see. Settle down in front of the stone, and make sure you are comfortable as you'll be in this position for a while. Take a few long, deep breaths to center yourself and still your mind.

2 Fix your gaze on a central point on the crystal. Breathe deeply and imagine that you are connecting with the stone. As you exhale, imagine you are releasing any tension from your body until you are fully relaxed.

3 Without moving your eyes, let your view expand to the outer rims of the crystal. This shouldn't be forced; think of it as a gentle expansion of awareness. Continue to hold your focus and breathe deeply. Over time, you might notice a shimmering field of energy around the crystal. Continue to relax and let the aura take shape.

4 Notice the color of the aura around the crystal. It might appear clear, silver, or white at first, but as you continue to gaze, you might see other hues coming through. When you are ready, focus your stare on the center of the stone once more and take a couple of deep, reviving breaths. You could close your eyes for a few seconds as you break contact with the crystal's energy.

5 Make some notes about your reading. Record any observations, feelings, or thoughts that you had, how easy or difficult you found this practice, and also what you saw. This will help you track your aura-reading progress.

BODY READING TIPS

Within this chapter you have discovered some of the most popular body reading techniques and how they work. These practices provide physical cues and clues that will help you tune in intuitively. Reading the body is an easy way to gain insights, particularly if you're interested in someone's character and general attitude to life. It's also a psychic art form that you can practice on yourself and those close to you. Here are some key tips and suggestions that will help you perfect this type of reading and also protect you psychically when reading for others.

Tune in

Take some time to tune in to your psychic mind before you begin. If you're reading for someone else, take a moment to breathe and imagine a connection forming between you. It helps if you visualize this as a stream of light that passes information from the querent to you through your intuition.

Be open to the little things

When reading for someone else, be open to any thoughts or feelings that surface as you sit in their presence. For example, a niggling feeling or an ache or pain that springs up unannounced and is unusual to you could be something that you are picking up from the other person. If something feels strange and alien to you, it's likely that it is coming from the querent. If you're practicing body reading on yourself, you might suddenly become aware of an emotion or have a random thought that pops into your head. This is your intuition speaking to you.

Explain your findings

If you're reading for someone else, it can be hard to know where to begin. Body reading is unlike any other form of divination. The querent doesn't pull a selection of cards like they might if they were having a tarot reading. They don't select rune stones or throw sticks, which would provide a starting point. Instead, you have to rely on your instincts and what you see—start by fully explaining the process and what you are going to do, then go on to outline your findings.

Dissolve your connection

Just as you have taken the time to establish a psychic connection with the querent, be sure to disconnect so that you don't carry any energy residue with you. A simple way of doing this is to visualize the connection gently fading away. You might also want to burn some sage oil or a sage smudge stick to cleanse yourself and the area around you of any negative energy.

Doing something physical at the end of a reading is a good idea. This takes you out of your intuitive mind and puts you in a present state. Sipping a glass of water or performing a few easy stretches are other ways to help to break the connection.

CHAPTER FIVE

CARTOMANCY: TAROT and ORACLE CARDS

In this chapter, you will learn about cartomancy, which is fortune-telling with cards, primarily tarot and oracle cards. The images on the cards are interpreted to form the basis of the reading.

An introduction to cartomancy

Cartomancy, or card reading, can be performed using a set of tarot or oracle cards, both of which can provide insight and guidance. This chapter introduces you to these two card types and explores the ways in which you can work with the cards in your divination practice. Both types of card feature specific images and themes that you can use to make your predictions, and many people collect tarot and oracle decks for their decorative qualities. While you don't have to have special psychic skills to read the cards, working with them can help to hone your intuition.

Usually, the reader will shuffle the cards and then pick a number of cards for chosen positions within a reading. These cards will then be deciphered together to create a picture of the current situation and offer insight for the future. If the reading is for someone else, the reader might ask the querent to handle the deck and then choose a number of cards for each position.

Who does it work for?

Card reading is a wonderful way for anyone to develop their psychic senses. This is a fun and imaginative practice that helps the reader tap into their intuition by using powerful images and symbols that stimulate the subconscious mind. If you're a visual person who thinks in pictures, this will appeal to you, and if you're particularly artistic you'll appreciate the images and find recalling their meaning easy.

An ancient form of divination, card reading has fascinated humankind for centuries, mainly because it works with symbols that resonate with many belief systems. If you enjoy building narratives and you're an adept storyteller then you will find card reading, particularly the tarot, an enjoyable practice.

Early techniques

Cartomancy emerged in Europe around the fourteenth century with the invention of the first set of playing cards in the 1360s. While initially the cards were used for gaming purposes, the intricacy of the patterns and the different suits triggered the imagination, and soon cards were being drawn to reveal a person's fate.

Over time, this evolved, and a new suit of cards was added to the existing set. Created in Italy and known as the Trionfi, these cards were more powerful than the original four suits and considered the "trumps" of the deck. They were illustrated with colorful caricatures inspired by medieval reenactments of Roman processions and also contained the character of *il Matto*, now recognized as "The Fool" card in the tarot. Over the years, "trumps" evolved into a fortune-telling game, and the cards transformed to accommodate this new purpose.

DID YOU KNOW?

Cartomancy became hugely popular in the eighteenth century, in part thanks to French occultist Jean-Baptiste Alliette, who went by the name Etteilla, which is his surname spelled backward. Etteilla is considered to be the first professional tarot reader. He wrote books on the subject, founded a tarot society, and designed his own tarot deck, versions of which are still in use around the world today.

Protection ritual

Reading the cards can expose you to psychic energy. This is particularly true with tarot cards because they deal with ancient symbols that can be portals into the spirit world. If you're reading for other people, you'll likely pick up on how they are feeling, and this can affect your mood and leave you feeling drained. To avoid this pitfall, it's a good idea to perform a protection ritual before you start. This will prepare you psychically, so that you feel confident opening up to the spiritual realm and connecting with the energy around you.

You will need: Some space to work and a piece of smoky quartz or obsidian (pictured below, top to bottom), both of which are associated with protection and will balance your energy.

1   Sit in your space and take a moment to center yourself. Breathe deeply and appreciate the stillness, allowing time for your body and mind settle.

2   Hold your stone of choice close to your heart chakra, which is situated in the center of your chest.

3   As you breathe in, imagine you're absorbing the powerful grounding energy of the crystal.

4   As you exhale, visualize a stream of white light pouring from your heart chakra. This light sweeps outward in a circular direction.

5   See the light form a circle around you. You might visualize this as a shimmering white light or, if you prefer, see a circle of fire in your mind.

6 For every breath, the circle of light gets stronger and brighter, and you reinforce this image in your mind.

7 To finish, say in a loud and confident voice "Circle of light, protect me as I work, keep my energy safe and secure, so that I can reach out fully with my psychic senses."

Know that this circle of protection you have created will repel any negative energy, keeping you safe and centered during your readings.

An alternative to visualizing a protective circle of energy would be to create a physical circle, using a selection of small crystals, to outline the space you work in. Stones such as obsidian and smoky quartz are ideal for this, but you could also use a mixture, including regular quartz for positive energy and amethyst to amplify your psychic skills.

Tarot cards

Best for: Creative souls who enjoy storytelling and symbolism, and those who think visually.

What are they?

Tarot cards combine powerful images with symbols that trigger the psyche. A standard tarot deck contains 78 cards, divided into two groups: the Major Arcana (22 cards) and the Minor Arcana (56 cards). Each card has a specific meaning that can be interpreted alone or alongside others. Cards are often arranged in particular layouts, known as spreads, with each position representing a different aspect of a question or situation.

A gateway to self-discovery, the tarot gives a picture of where you are in your life right now and offers an insight into issues and trends that might have an influence on future events. A fortune-telling tool that started life as a parlor game for those with money and status, the origins of the cards are somewhat sketchy. Some believed that the roots of this mystical art came from ancient Egypt, but it's now apparent that the tarot started life as a "trumps"-style card game and was invented in Italy. The practice then spread across Europe by the Romani people who traditionally traveled from place to place and used the cards for divination purposes.

Types of tarot cards

One of the most famous decks in the history of divination is the Rider Waite Smith Tarot Deck. This was created by the academic and mystic Arthur Edward Waite and illustrated by Pamela Colman Smith, a gifted artist and psychic. Both Waite and Smith were members of the esoteric society Golden Dawn. Together, they created a tarot deck that would form the basis of many others to come. The potent imagery on each card was intertwined with powerful, mystical symbols, and the narratives held within made the cards easy to understand and interpret.

Those new to the tarot often find the Rider Waite Smith deck one of the simplest to work with. That said, there are thousands of different types of decks, covering a range of themes and artistic styles. For example, there are decks associated with mythologies, faeries, and witches, alongside animal-themed cards. It's important to pick one that resonates with you on some level. The artwork should also be considered because you will be working in depth and at length with your cards, so you need to choose images that you're comfortable with and enjoy looking at. A selection of cards from different tarot decks is shown below, details of which can be found on page 144.

The Major Arcana

In a standard 78-card tarot deck, the Major Arcana makes up 22 cards. These cards have a powerful influence on us—they are generally considered to be the cards of fate because they cover the big life-changing moments that we all experience during our journey on the Earth. Packed with wisdom, they provide a deeper insight into our hopes, fears, and motivations.

The Major Arcana cards follow a narrative structure, which begins with the central character of The Fool. The journey then charts The Fool's progress as he navigates the twists and turns of life and learns about himself and his place in the world. While these cards have designated themes, it's important to develop your own relationship with each one. Here is a brief outline of what each card represents to get you started.

0 The Fool: A free spirit with an open heart and mind, The Fool is about to embark on a life-changing journey. When this card appears, it's a sign that you are about to begin a new adventure. Fresh starts are well-starred, but there's an element of risk, too. This card says "Have fun and enjoy this new beginning, but don't be naive and rush in blindly!"

I The Magician: This card highlights the skills and talents you have at your disposal. It's a reminder that you are uniquely gifted, and that you have everything you need to manifest your desired outcome. This card says "Be bold, embrace your talents, and be the author of your story."

II The High Priestess: Also known as the divine feminine, The High Priestess is the mistress of mystery. A wise and intuitive woman, she represents your inner wisdom and the subconscious mind. She is synonymous with psychic power and signifies a period of withdrawal, as you go within for hidden knowledge. This card says "Trust your intuition; you have all the answers you seek."

III The Empress: The nurturing influence of The Empress can be felt in all things. Synonymous with Mother Nature, this card embodies fertility and new growth and suggests the birth of an idea and a particularly creative period ahead. This card says "Unleash your imagination and let your creativity flow."

IV The Emperor: This card represents a father figure; someone who has a degree of authority and power. When The Emperor appears in a reading, this suggests the querent has reached the stage in life where they feel in control and can take the lead. This card says "Step into your power; you are in control."

V The Hierophant: A card of tradition, The Hierophant often represents a spiritual guide or religious teacher. This card is synonymous with rules, customs, and religious practices. When The Hierophant card appears, it can mean that the querent is exploring their spirituality. This card says "Seek advice or counsel if you are unsure about the way forward."

VI The Lovers: A card of love and relationships, this card symbolizes the passion of two people coming together. It can signify the start of a relationship, or that the querent has met their soulmate. Equally, it can be about decisions and life choices. This card says "Trust your heart and let it lead the way."

VII The Chariot: A card of focused action, The Chariot suggests a time of movement and progress for the querent; they have made a decision, and now they are implementing their skills to make it work. This card says "You have the drive to succeed, so go for it!"

VIII Justice: A symbol of truth and fairness, Justice is synonymous with balance and acting fairly. It suggests that whatever is happening now is a result of actions taken in the past. It can also refer to legal matters and is a positive sign that things will go well. This card says "Be fair in your treatment of others and maintain balance and order."

IX The Hermit: The card of the loner, The Hermit usually appears when there is the need for solitude and solace. Stillness is key at this time. The querent must disconnect from the noise and find peace within through meditation and other soothing practices. This card says "Be still; take the time you need to recharge."

X The Wheel of Fortune: The cycles of life are represented by The Wheel of Fortune. Synonymous with change and destiny, this card relates to the highs and lows of life and can indicate a swift change in fortune for the querent. This card says "Embrace the highs and stay positive during the lows; the wheel of fate is always turning."

XI Strength: When Strength appears in a reading, it's a clear indicator that the querent has the strength and resilience to achieve anything. Synonymous with tenacity and compassion, this card can also relate to a period of health and vitality. This card says "You have inner reserves of strength; tap into them."

XII The Hanged Man: This card relates to a period of stagnation, a pause when things will remain as they are. The Hanged Man is synonymous with sacrifice and suggests that the querent may need to give something up in order to move forward. This card says "Be patient; use this pause to reflect on where you are and where you would like to be."

XIII Death: This might seem like an ominous card, but it's the chance for a new beginning. Death indicates that a door may be closing—there could be an ending of sorts—but with it comes the chance to wipe the slate clean and start again. This card says "Let go of the past; it is time to move on and make a fresh start."

XIV Temperance: This card suggests a period of peace and balance. The querent will find the harmony they seek by having patience with themselves and with others. Synonymous with purpose, Temperance is a gentle card associated with calmness. This card says "All things in moderation; be patient and let things unfold at their own pace."

XV The Devil: The card of restraint, The Devil is associated with temptation and addiction. It often relates to bad habits that need to be broken and cycles of behavior that are self-limiting. This card says "Be brave and break the chains that bind you."

XVI The Tower: Synonymous with chaos and destruction, The Tower appears in a reading to warn the querent that they are on unstable ground. They may be going through a period of upheaval and it's likely they'll feel vulnerable and confused. While it might seem like a negative influence, The Tower provides the opportunity to reinvent yourself and your life. This card says "Take a deep breath and see this as an awakening."

XVII The Star: The Star of hope shines brightly when this card appears in a reading. Connected with renewal, this card is all about optimism and is a positive sign for the future. It relates to inspiration, rebirth, and rejuvenation. This card says "You are about to step into the light; stay positive and hopeful."

XVIII The Moon: The light of the Moon makes everything look different, making this the card of illusion. The querent may not have all the facts and may be feeling emotional. Feelings may remain hidden or suddenly rise to the surface, and creativity will be in full flow. This card says "Everything is not as it seems; trust your instincts at this time."

XIX The Sun: When this card appears, the Sun is shining on every aspect of life. Joy and laughter abound, and there's likely to be a period of good fortune and prosperity. The querent is blessed with success and happiness. This card says "Be joyful and have fun; you are blessed."

XX Judgment: The breakthrough card, Judgment urges the querent to review their past choices and to emerge into the light. There's a sense of rejuvenation here, especially after a period of reflection. Judgment is synonymous with positive change and awakening. This card says "Step forward and be the best version of yourself."

XXI The World: The final card in the Major Arcana, The World is synonymous with fulfillment, success, and completion. The querent has achieved what they set out to do. They have reached the goal, and they can now revel in the rewards. This card says "You have the world at your feet; you have arrived!"

The Minor Arcana

Comprising 56 cards, the Minor Arcana is split into four suits—the Cups, Swords, Pentacles, and Wands—which are related to the four suits of a standard pack of playing cards. Each suit has a particular sphere of influence:

- **Cups** relate to the emotions and are associated with love, passion, joy, and fulfillment.

- **Swords** relate to actions and are synonymous with power, force, conflict, and change.

- **Pentacles**, also known as coins, relate to wealth. These cards are associated with financial matters, security, stability, and abundance.

- **Wands** represent communication. They are synonymous with ideas, enterprise, negotiation, and adventure.

Each suit is made up of ten number cards, Ace through Ten, and four "court" cards, which include the Page, Knight, Queen, and King. In some packs, the Page is changed to the Princess. The court cards often relate to a person in the querent's life, but they can also be a representation of some aspect of the querent. For example, the Queen of Swords is a dynamic woman who means business and she might appear if the querent is acting this way at the time of the reading.

While the Major Arcana tends to be associated with the larger, life-changing influences and events that might come along, the cards of the Minor Arcana provide insight into day-to-day dealings, those everyday occurrences that happen to all of us.

A brief outline of each card's meaning is provided on pages 112–115, but as with the Major Arcana, it's important to develop your own ideas based on how you feel about the card and its imagery and symbolism.

CUPS

Ace of Cups: Suggests the beginning of a love affair, a gift or token of affection, and feelings of love and affection between friends and family.

Two of Cups: Signifies two people making a commitment to each other—marriage or some other kind of union or romance.

Three of Cups: Related to celebration, happy times with those you love, and family gatherings.

Four of Cups: Linked to apathy, lethargy, feeling disenchanted with life, and lacking in focus.

Five of Cups: Associated with regret, disappointment, and a sense of loss.

Six of Cups: Signifies childhood memories, looking back to the past, and feeling nostalgic and sentimental.

Seven of Cups: Suggests confusion and having mixed feelings about something. There may be lots of options and the querent is overwhelmed.

Eight of Cups: Indicates a sense of abandonment, disconnection, withdrawal, and of leaving something behind.

Nine of Cups: Often considered the "wish card," because it is associated with manifestation. Also linked to fulfillment, satisfaction, and happiness.

Ten of Cups: Signifies harmony, joy, and dreams coming true.

Page of Cups: Related to being curious, openhearted, trusting your intuition, and following your heart. Can represent a child or young person.

Knight of Cups: Linked to creativity and charm. Also relates to a person who brings new ideas and inspiration into your life, who could possibly be a love interest.

Queen of Cups: Suggests a caring and empathic woman. The querent might be embodying this energy and taking on a nurturing role.

King of Cups: Indicates emotional maturity and having reached a state where you have mastered your feelings. Can represent an older father figure.

SWORDS

Ace of Swords: Indicates a breakthrough, out-of-the-blue action, or passionate spark.

Two of Swords: Represents indecision, being at some sort of stalemate or crossroads, or not being able to see clearly.

Three of Swords: Signifies heartache and heartbreak, feeling hurt and betrayed.

Four of Swords: Suggests recuperation and rest, taking time out or away from a difficult situation.

Five of Swords: Related to disagreements, arguments, conflict, and things not going your way.

Six of Swords: Associated with leaving something behind—an idea, behavior, or person—moving on, release, and healing.

Seven of Swords: Indicates some kind of deception, lies, or trickery.

Eight of Swords: Connected to feeling trapped or isolated, a sense of imprisonment, and wanting to break free.

Nine of Swords: Linked to anxiety, nightmares, fears surfacing, and worrying about anything and everything.

Ten of Swords: Resembles an ending of sorts, disruption, chaos, or destructive influences.

Page of Swords: Suggests a restless soul, feeling mentally alert, and full of new ideas. Can also represent a young, intelligent person.

Knight of Swords: Indicates an ambitious person; this could be the querent or someone in their life. Also linked to feeling driven and focused.

Queen of Swords: Represents an intellectual woman who has clear judgment and knows what she wants. This card symbolizes both wisdom and logic combined.

King of Swords: Embodies a powerful and astute individual—the querent might have stepped into this role and is acting with authority.

PENTACLES

Ace of Pentacles: Associated with a new beginning in relation to finances, manifesting abundance, and the opportunity for prosperity.

Two of Pentacles: Relates to balance and flexibility, seeing both sides and maintaining your position, particularly when it comes to finances.

Three of Pentacles: Signals teamwork and collaboration, working together to create something new. This is a card of cooperation.

Four of Pentacles: Represents greed; also holding on to money through fear of losing everything.

Five of Pentacles: Linked to insecurity and financial loss; can indicate that the querent needs to be resilient.

Six of Pentacles: Symbolizes material security, abundance, sharing wealth, and generous gifts.

Seven of Pentacles: Embodies steady progress and perseverance, seeing a light at the end of the tunnel, and accruing money.

Eight of Pentacles: Suggests a period of hard work and effort, mastering your craft. Can signify an apprenticeship or a training course.

Nine of Pentacles: Linked to self-sufficiency, success and achieving goals, financial security, abundance, and recognition of past efforts.

Ten of Pentacles: Indicates a prosperous time, money flowing in, family riches, and all the benefits of a good life.

Page of Pentacles: Resembles a financial opportunity, tapping into your potential, and trying to manifest new goals.

Knight of Pentacles: Represents striving for a goal or financial security, hard work, and effort. Can also refer to a businessman.

Queen of Pentacles: Embodies a down-to-earth, driven woman; also suggests motherhood or a mother figure. A card of stability and strength.

King of Pentacles: Associated with wealth and abundance and a man who creates his own success. This card is related to leadership.

WANDS

Ace of Wands: Associated with the spark of an idea, a new invention, or a burst of inspiration.

Two of Wands: Relates to a business partnership or enterprise; two people coming together to work on a new venture.

Three of Wands: Signals a period of productivity, expansion, and new adventures. Often linked to travel or going on a journey.

Four of Wands: Indicates stability and unity. This card symbolizes joy and success and can indicate family gatherings and celebrations.

Five of Wands: Signifies disagreements and problems with communication. There could be arguments and obstacles ahead.

Six of Wands: A card of victory and great success, which suggests a sense of accomplishment and reward for hard work.

Seven of Wands: Indicates that there are challenges ahead and you may have to stand up for what you believe in.

Eight of Wands: Symbolizes energy, activity, and alignment. Suggests a period of industry, making new connections, and broadening horizons.

Nine of Wands: Courage is needed when this card appears. There may be a test of faith or a final challenge ahead.

Ten of Wands: Represents feeling weighed down with responsibility or burdened in some way; taking on more than you can actually do.

Page of Wands: A free spirit who has a curious mind, this card represents inspiration.

Knight of Wands: Signifies vitality, enthusiasm, and pursuing your passion. This can represent a confident and ambitious person in the querent's life.

Queen of Wands: Indicates a warm, confident person; someone who is outgoing and friendly with everyone.

King of Wands: Resembles a visionary leader who inspires others. This is a powerful person and often represents an entrepreneur. It can mean that the querent is stepping into this role.

Reading tarot cards step-by-step

1 Create the perfect atmosphere for your reading by marking out some sacred space. You can do this by burning sage to cleanse the area, lighting scented candles and incense, and arranging an array of crystals, such as amethyst and quartz, to promote psychic awareness. Some readers like to lay their cards on a satin scarf or a particular piece of material to enhance the reading further.

2 Sit in stillness for a moment to calm your mind. Inhale deeply and follow the breath on its journey through your body. As you exhale, imagine you are releasing any tension and negative energy.

3 Shuffle the cards while you are in a relaxed state of mind. If you're reading for yourself, it's important to connect with the cards through touch. If you're reading for another person, you might want to ask them to shuffle the cards so that they connect fully with the deck.

4 Clear your workspace so that there are no obstacles and you can arrange the cards in the correct reading positions for the chosen spread (see the next page). Be sure to familiarize yourself with these positions and what they mean in advance. This helps the reading to be fluent and allows your psychic skills to shine through.

5 Draw the cards when you are ready and lay them out in front of you. Consider not only the meaning of the cards you have chosen (see pages 106–115) and the positions they are in, but also what they mean to you. Connect with the colorful images and let them permeate your mind.

6 Take note of any thoughts and feelings that arise during the reading. The cards provide a portal from which you can tune in to your intuitive mind.

Three-card spread

A spread is an arrangement of cards—the reader interprets the meaning of each card and its position in the spread. There are lots of spreads to try but a three-card spread is a good starting point. It can offer an overview of the past, present, and future or answer a specific query.

You will need: A deck of tarot cards.

1 To begin, shuffle the cards thoroughly while thinking about what you'd like to know. You may have a specific theme, focus, or issue.

2 When you're ready, use your left hand (which is closely linked to your heart and your intuitive side) to split the cards into three piles, with the cards facing down.

3 Now pick a pile that you are drawn to. Remove the other two piles then spread the chosen pile of cards out using your left hand.

4 Take a minute to still your mind then choose three cards at random and turn them face up, one at a time.

   • The first card relates to the past. If you're dealing with a specific issue then this card could explain how the issue began.

   • The second card relates to the present—where you are now and how you are feeling.

   • The third card relates to your future. This card represents the best possible outcome at the moment. This is not set in stone—it depends on what action you take from this point onward—but it's a good indication of whether your future is well-starred if you continue on the same path.

5 If you need further clarity, draw a final card. This represents any influences around you at the moment that could be relevant.

  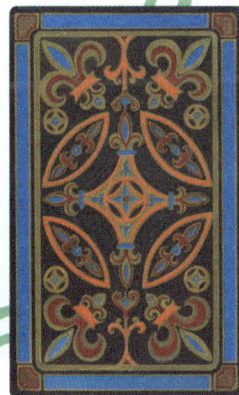

1 PAST   2 PRESENT   3 FUTURE

Manifesting with tarot cards

While tarot is primarily about predicting events and trends, and tapping into your inner wisdom, it can also be used to shape the future. This might seem at odds with divination but is, in fact, a key part because it relies on a deep knowledge of the cards, the symbols and meanings, and the ability to foresee and manifest through potent visions.

Once you have mastered reading the cards and feel comfortable with their meanings, have a go at using the Major Arcana to shape the future. This will not only help to develop your psychic skills through visualization, but it will also help you connect with each of the cards on a personal level.

You will need: The Major Arcana cards from a tarot deck, a candle, and some time and space to relax.

1   Light the candle and spend a few minutes focusing on the flame to quieten your mind.

2   Lay the full set of Major Arcana cards out in front of you so that you can see each one clearly.

3   Begin by thinking about what you'd like to manifest. Start with something small, for example, perhaps you have felt stuck in life or that things are not moving on the career front.

4   Select the card that resonates the most with what you are trying to manifest (refer to pages 106–110 for the meanings of each card) and hold it in both hands. In this example, you could select The Chariot, which is associated with movement and work, and depicts a time of activity and achievement.

5 Connect with the image on the card and let it permeate your mind.

6 Close your eyes and visualize the image. Try and retain all of the details then imagine the card as a portrait that you are looking at.

7 Imagine the portrait is getting bigger, and that with each breath it becomes more lifelike. When the picture is big enough, step into it so that you become a part of the scene.

8 Breathe deeply and take in the invigorating energy of the card. Say "As I see, so it is. My energy connects with this!"

9 Step back out of the card and let the image reduce down in your mind. Slowly open your eyes and look at the card once more.

10 Place the card somewhere prominent in your home, so that you will see it every day and be reminded of its meaning.

Oracle cards

Best for: Beginners and those wanting to develop and practice their intuitive skills.

What are they?

A modern invention, oracle cards are specially designed cards that have images and symbols with a range of meanings. Used mainly to tap into inner wisdom and for guidance, oracle cards are the perfect tool for self-reflection and provide daily insights and predictions. The reader can select a card at any given time and use it as a prompt to contemplate or read its meaning and harness the energy of the card. Sometimes, more than one card will be drawn, depending on the querent's situation. For example, seven cards could be selected to represent the days of the upcoming week.

Types of oracle cards

Oracle cards come in all shapes and sizes. Unlike tarot cards, there is no set format to the arrangement of the deck—there can be any number of cards in a pack depending on the author, but usually fewer than in a tarot deck. The cards often reflect a theme or mythology and there any many different options available, such as angel-themed cards, Celtic-influenced decks, and cards that represent animal totems. It's important to work with a deck that resonates with you. Readers tend to feel drawn to a particular set depending on their interests, spirituality, or preference of artwork.

Reading oracle cards step-by-step

1   Create a sacred space for your oracle card reading. You can do this by clearing a table and laying a cloth on the surface, arranging crystals in a circle, lighting a scented candle, or simply by burning your favorite incense. If you're wanting to develop your intuitive skills, it's important to allow yourself time and to mark the occasion, rather than dipping into the deck while you're on the move or busy doing something else.

2   Handle the pack for at least a couple of minutes. This will help you connect with the cards. As you do this, think about any issues or questions you might have.

3   Lay the cards face down on the reading surface and spread them out. Take a deep breath to calm your mind, then pick a card. You can select more than one if you feel it's necessary for your situation.

4   Gaze at the image on the card. Let any thoughts flow through your mind. You might instinctively know what this card means to you, but allow any intuitive insights to come through by sitting with it in the moment and appreciating the image. Notice any feelings that surface at this time.

5   Consider the meaning and think about it in terms of your own situation. Does it make sense? Can you see what the card is telling you? Even if it doesn't resonate with you now, make a note of it, either mentally or on paper, because the meaning may present itself over time.

Make your own oracle deck

There are thousands of oracle decks in existence, but why not create your own? This is a great way to tune into your subconscious mind, develop psychic skills, and exercise your creativity. You don't have to be arty to make this work. All you need is a little inspiration and the time and space to work on your designs.

You will need: A set of note cards, art supplies (such as glitter, glue, paint, pens, markers), gift paper and tape, some paper on which to write your ideas down, and something to keep your cards in.

1   To begin, have a brainstorming session to come up with ideas for your cards. Think about themes that appeal to you, such as flowers and plants, birds, or symbols. Anything goes at this stage so be as imaginative as you like and make a list of your ideas, then pick a theme from your list that resonates with you the most.

2 Decide how many cards you would like to include in your deck then select this number of note cards. The back of the card is usually uniform, so take the gift paper and cover one side of each card with this, either taping or gluing it in position.

3 Now you can begin to illustrate the front side of each card. Have fun with this. You can draw the images yourself or, if you struggle with drawing, cut pictures from magazines. You could keep it simple with shapes and patterns, or be as intricate as you like. Decorate your cards with anything you have to hand—for example, you could use stickers, glitter, or silver paper. This is your chance to be inventive.

4 Once you have completed the set, take the time to sit with each card. Gaze at the images you have created and consider how they make you feel. Listen to your intuition and let it direct you to the specific meaning of each card.

5 Make a note of each interpretation for future reference, then safely store the cards away.

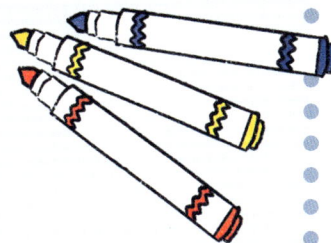

CARTOMANCY TIPS

This chapter covers the two main types of cards that you can use in divination. Oracle cards are a good starting point because they stimulate the imagination and help you tap into your intuition. There are usually fewer cards in an oracle deck and the meanings are more straightforward than with tarot cards. Tarot is a mystical art form that has fascinated people for centuries. It offers multilayered readings and the opportunity to gain self-knowledge. Here you will find tips and suggestions to help you master both.

Connect on a deeper level

Whichever type of cards you use, you need to form a personal connection with them. This happens naturally over time, but to help you on the way, take each card and sit with it for a while. Connect with the images and symbol and notice how you feel as you hold the card. Ask yourself "What does this mean to me?" You may notice details within the image that leap out at you. Often, readers say they pick up on different elements depending on who they are reading for.

Visualize each card

Once you are familiar with each card, connect with it at random times of the day. Sit in stillness for a couple of minutes and bring the image of the card to mind. Make the colors more vivid and increase the size. Notice every little detail. This strengthens the connection you have with the card.

Tell a story

Remember that when deciphering the cards, particularly the tarot, you are making narrative connections and interpreting the selected cards together using the structure of a specific reading, therefore it helps to practice your storytelling skills. Draw out random cards and place them in a line, then have a go at telling a story using each card as a prompt. This will help you advance to more complex types of reading.

Practice, practice, practice

Like any skill, reading the cards takes time to master. You can't expect to pick up an oracle or tarot deck and instantly connect with it. It can take many months of practice before you are adept and ready to read for another person. Taking into account the other tips listed will give you a helping hand, but there is no short cut, particularly if you choose to work with the tarot. Accept that you will need a degree of patience and a learning period and enjoy getting to know the secrets of the cards and developing your psychic awareness.

CHAPTER SIX

TASSEOMANCY: TEA LEAVES AND COFFEE GROUNDS

Tasseomancy is the ancient practice of interpreting the patterns and shapes formed by tea leaves and coffee grounds to make a prediction.

An introduction to tasseomancy

The word "tasseomancy" originates from the French word *tasse* (meaning "cup") and the Greek word *mancy* (meaning "divination"). Easily accessible and popular, reading tea leaves and coffee grounds is a fun way of predicting the future and tapping into the psyche. The reader makes a cup of the querent's favorite brew, using either loose-leaf tea or coffee grounds, with the intention of divination. The querent drinks the liquid, leaving some in the bottom of the cup so that there is residue left behind. The reader swirls the cup and its contents, usually in a clockwise direction two or three times, to let the leaves or grounds settle. The reader then gazes into the cup and interprets any shapes and patterns that have formed by the remaining leaves or grounds. This ancient divination practice started as a form of entertainment for the higher classes but remains popular to this day thanks to the universal love of a brew.

Who does it work for?

This type of intuitive reading can be done by anyone who is open and psychically aware. It takes some creative flair and a degree of confidence to recognize shapes and symbols and build a picture from this, but once you get into the habit of extending your awareness and engaging the imagination, it becomes a natural skill.

There's an element of fun to reading tea leaves and coffee grounds. It's a great option for those who favor a more informal type of divination, and those who want to flex their intuitive skills daily. What can start as a game to stimulate the imagination can soon become uncannily accurate and a way of accessing inner wisdom and guidance.

Early techniques

The tradition of tea leaf reading began in ancient China, with the invention of loose-leaf tea. According to legend, the Chinese emperor Shen Nung first discovered tea in 2737 BCE and little did he know that it would become a favorite beverage and an important fortune-telling tool. The practice of tea leaf reading soon became popular in China and the Middle East. When tea was brought to England and Europe in the Victorian era, tea leaf reading became a popular parlor game for the upper echelons of society. The game was known as "throwing cups," thanks to the process of flinging the remaining tea away to read the patterns left by the loose leaves.

The roots of reading coffee grounds stem from the Ottoman Empire. While the first coffee beans are thought to have been cultivated in Ethiopia, the practice of brewing was first popularized in Istanbul, Turkey. Palace wives and members of Sultan Suleiman's harem were banned from frequenting coffee houses outside of the palace so these women would instead gather to drink Turkish coffee and were visited by a *falci* (a type of fortune teller or psychic medium) who would join them for coffee and then read their grounds.

Types of tea and coffee readings

Many readers have a special cup or teapot that they use solely for readings. The shape and style of cup or mug can have an influence on the reading. A small, shallow cup offers a quick insight into the querent's situation and is more likely to reflect the immediate future, while a large, deep cup provides an in-depth reading. Whatever choice of cup or mug, make sure it's fairly wide-brimmed and a light shade, so that you can clearly see the shapes emerge.

The type of tea can be tailored to the querent's question or state of mind. Black tea is associated with strength and protection—if the querent is feeling vulnerable, this is a good choice. Green tea is synonymous with new growth and abundance and works well with those looking for a fresh start, while white tea is linked to peace and purity.

Turkish coffee is often used in coffee readings because it leaves a lot of residue, but any type of filtered, ground coffee works well.

Third eye ritual

This type of reading relies solely on psychic ability and your artistic skills. You'll need to feel relaxed and open so that you can connect and interpret the symbols presented to you. The following ritual will open and clear your third eye chakra, which is the energy center associated with psychic energy. This will help to expand your awareness so that you can tune in effectively while also allowing your creativity to flow.

You will need: Lavender essential oil, sweet almond oil, a small bowl, cushions and throws, a pillow, and somewhere quiet to relax.

1   Create a sacred and safe space where you can relax. Arrange cushions and throws, and a pillow for your head.

2   Add a tablespoon of sweet almond oil to the bowl then mix in three drops of lavender essential oil, which will relax and stimulate the psychic senses.

3   Dip your index finger into the oil mixture and gently draw a circle in the middle of your forehead, which is where the third eye chakra is located.

4   Lie down with your head supported and trace a circle over this area once more.

5   Close your eyes and relax fully, with your arms by your sides. Breathe deeply and focus your attention on the area in the center of your forehead.

6   Imagine that you have a third eye located in this spot. Currently, it's closed, but each time you release a breath, the eyelid begins to open until gradually the eye is revealed.

7   When the eye is fully open, visualize a stream of purple light emanating from this area. This illuminating light casts its brightness far and wide so that you can see and sense the unseen.

8   Say "My third eye is open; my awareness is keen. Intuition flows through me; I see the unseen."

Tasseomancy step-by-step

1 Set your intention before you begin. Think about any areas of interest or issues that you need help with, and how deeply you would like to look into the future. This is not your normal morning brew; this is an opportunity to connect with your subconscious and receive intuitive guidance.

2 Prepare your reading cup or mug. You could cleanse it with boiling water and herbs, or by leaving it under the light of the Moon overnight. Make sure the cup or mug is clean before you begin. You could use a saucer to catch any excess liquid once most of the tea has been drunk.

3 Relax and breathe deeply as your drink brews, then sip and enjoy it. Be aware that you need to drink most, but not all, of the liquid before you can do a reading. Once consumed, swirl the remaining liquid and turn the cup over onto the saucer to let the liquid drain for a few seconds. Turn the cup back upright and you are ready to begin the reading.

4 Focus your mind and soften your gaze. Look at the patterns and shapes made by the leaves or grounds. Treat each image as a symbol and reflect on what it means to you. You might see more than one symbol within the cup—allow yourself to fully contemplate the symbols and consider their deeper meaning. Turn to pages 135–137 for some common symbols and their possible meanings.

5 Take your time. Reading tea leaves or coffee grounds cannot be rushed. Give yourself free license to daydream and connect with the images. Let any thoughts, feelings, or insights arise. It's a good idea to keep your divination journal at your side so that you can make notes.

6 Have fun! If you want to improve your tasseomancy skills, invite your family and friends over and practice reading their tea leaves or coffee grounds.

Herbal magic

If you're not a fan of tea or coffee, or if you want to enhance your predictions and give them a magical twist, you can use a herbal infusion instead. Herbs have an abundance of properties, which will enrich your reading experience and boost psychic awareness.

For example, rosemary is synonymous with clarity and vision, sage will cleanse and purify, while parsley helps to boost personal power and psychic awareness. Chamomile is relaxing and will help you connect with your intuition.

You will need: Fresh herbs of your choice, a chopping knife, a pan with boiling water, a colander, a cup, honey, and a spoon.

1 Take a handful of your chosen herbs and chop them up finely.

2 Place the chopped herbs in the bottom of the pan of boiling water and let the herbs simmer for at least five minutes.

3 Once the liquid has simmered, remove the bulk of the herbs (the stems etc.) and use the colander to strain the liquid into the cup.

4 Add a spoonful of honey to sweeten, if necessary.

5 Sip and savor your herbal concoction while letting it infuse your body and mind.

6 When you've finished, swirl the remaining residue in the bottom of the cup and look at any patterns created. As with any form of tasseomancy, you'll need to relax and let images and symbols appear and then decipher them.

If you don't wish to drink your herbal concoction, you can inhale the aromatic steam. This will help you reap the psychic benefits of each herb. After a couple of minutes, throw the remaining liquid away, leaving some residue at the bottom of the cup. Turn the residue into a clean bowl and perform your reading by looking at the shapes the herbs make.

Positioning and prediction

It is important to consider where each image or symbol sits within the cup because this can have an influence on the prediction.

- Symbols that fall to the left of the cup tend to relate to the past while symbols that fall to the right are usually associated with the future.

- Symbols near the rim of the cup are synonymous with the immediate future, while those that are positioned toward the base of the cup relate to deeper issues that may come to the surface as events unfold.

- Some readers take into account the liquid left in the bottom of the cup. If there are bubbles in it, then this is seen as a positive sign and can indicate an unexpected windfall or surprise, whereas dregs that form liquid lumps are seen as obstacles and challenges ahead.

Create a symbol directory

As you develop your tea leaf or coffee ground reading skills, you'll begin to recognize certain images and symbols. At this point it's a good idea to create a personal directory of what each one means. Some symbols are universal, and so the meaning is straightforward, but others relate directly to your personal experience and are unique to you as the reader.

  If you're artistic, you might want to draw the symbols as you see them and then log the meaning, but a written record is equally useful. All you need is a notebook and plenty of space to write your definitions and thoughts.

Symbols and their meanings

To help you get started, here's a list of some of the symbols you might see along with their corresponding meanings.

Airplane: Relates to travel, possibly overseas, and can also represent a visitor from afar.

Anchor: Associated with stability and feeling secure and grounded. If this symbol appears, it could suggest that the querent feels stuck.

Arrow: Symbolizing movement and progress, an arrow can indicate that the querent needs to take targeted action.

Axe: Indicates hard work and putting in the effort to reap the rewards. An axe suggests that the querent may need to keep chipping away and working at something.

Ball: This can represent a sporting activity, or that the querent is athletic. It also suggests that they are playing a game in some area of their life.

Belt: Signifies feeling trapped in some way. A belt suggests limitations that have been placed on the querent, and having to abide by the rules.

Bird: Synonymous with freedom, the ability to soar above the clouds, and to see things from a different perspective. Birds can also indicate a time of success and prosperity.

Car: Relates to movement and travel. If a car appears, this could mean that a small journey will be significant for the querent.

Cat: An independent spirit, the cat also relates to playfulness and a need to explore. A cat is synonymous with adventure.

Cup: Represents an offering or a gift, which could be physical or spiritual. A cup also suggests abundance.

Dog: Signifies a loyal and faithful companion or friend. This symbol also relates to friendship and love.

Dragon: The querent may be about to embark on a passionate affair or they might have dangerous encounters in the future.

Flower: Linked to happiness and joy, a flower also represents new growth and creativity.

Fox: This symbol is synonymous with resourcefulness. It also suggests the querent may need to have their wits about them.

Heart: Associated with love, romance, and affection. The bigger and clearer the heart appears, the deeper the love connection.

Horse: Indicates slow, steady progress. If the querent is facing a challenge or trying to reach a goal, this is a sign that, with patience and perseverance, they will succeed.

House: Synonymous with family life and the home, this symbol could suggest moving house or home improvements. It also relates to security.

Key: Relates to new opportunities and discoveries. A key can indicate the unlocking of potential and the querent stepping into their power.

Moon: A symbol that relates to the intuition and psychic development, the Moon can indicate illusion and mystery—the querent isn't in full possession of the facts at this time.

Ocean: Represents a time of turbulent emotions and of change. The querent may experience erratic behavior.

Owl: A symbol of inner wisdom and guidance, the querent's intuition is finely tuned when this image appears.

Pen/Pencil: Synonymous with writing and creativity, this symbol is associated with inspiration and the spark of an idea.

Star: A sign that all will be well, the star is a symbol of hope and good fortune. It can also be related to fame.

Sun: This represents joy, happiness, and love. There may be celebrations and good times ahead.

Tree: A symbol related to growth in any area of life, a tree is also synonymous with strength and standing your ground.

World: The world is a symbol of completion and success. It suggests a sense of achievement and rewards for past efforts.

TASSEOMANCY TIPS

Reading tea leaves and coffee grounds is a technique that relies heavily on intuition. You need to be able to tune into your sixth sense and trust your instincts for this to work effectively. For those who are sensitive to energies, this is easy, but most of us need a little help to relax and go with the flow. The exercises outlined in this chapter will help you get into the right mindset and get started, but there are other tips and tricks that you can try to enhance your readings and build confidence.

Test yourself

Every day is an opportunity to use your intuition. Don't just wait for when you're doing a reading; flex your intuitive muscles at other times. For example, if you commute to work, you could imagine what the next person who gets on the bus, train, or tube will look like, and what they will be wearing, or you could pick a passenger and tune into them by guessing where they will get off.

If you like listening to the radio, guess the tunes before they come on, or what the DJ might say next. There are many ways that you can test and fine-tune your intuition.

Study symbols

If you want to perfect your tasseomancy skills, you need to become adept at recognizing symbols and understanding what they represent. Symbols come in all shapes and forms and can be found in many mythologies. Do some research—search the internet and scour books to develop an interest in different symbols and to learn more about their history and meanings.

Acknowledge your successes

Build confidence in your psychic abilities by acknowledging the progress you make along your journey. Keep a record of your readings that you can reflect on and, if you practice with other people, ask them for their feedback. You will notice that, over time, your success rate improves and your intuition becomes more heightened.

Have fun!

Reading tea leaves and coffee grounds is fun! It can be done in social situations with friends and family or when you have a quiet moment to yourself. This practice engages the imagination and allows you to see the magic in everyday routines.

Summary

Divination may seem mystical, but in truth it's a simple practice that anyone can try. All it takes is an open mind and the capacity to trust your intuition. There is no enigma here. Psychic ability is like any skill; it can be learned and fine-tuned if you are prepared to work at it. It's a case of finding the type of divination that appeals to you and fits with your skillset. For example, if you're a naturally visual person, then cartomancy (pages 98–125) is likely to resonate with you, because of the captivating images on the cards. If you have an ordered, logical mind, you might prefer an established numeric or alphabetic system, such as the runes (pages 54–61) or dice casting (pages 68–71).

Once you find a technique that works for you, the next step is to practice and exercise those intuitive muscles. If you want to excel, then a little effort is required. Like any type of learning, you need to make time for it and build it into your schedule. Get your friends and family involved and go on a journey of exploration. Learn as much as you can and engage with others who can help you, but most importantly, enjoy the experience because, when we have fun doing something, we absorb more information and connect with the world around us.

Divination might at first appear somber and serious, but it is not to be feared. It's something that we, as humans, have been doing for thousands of years, so—be brave, be bold, and begin your psychic adventure!

Glossary

Astragalomancy A form of divination using dice or small bones.

Aura The energy field that surrounds the body. Everyone has an aura, but they vary greatly in color, shape, and brightness.

Capnomancy Another term for smoke scrying, which is divination by reading and deciphering images within the smoke from a flame.

Cartomancy Divination by means of a deck of cards, usually tarot or oracle cards.

Chakras The body's energy centers. There are seven main chakras: crown, third eye, throat, heart, solar plexus, sacral, and root/base.

Chiromancy *See Palmistry.*

Cleansing The process of purifying a space or object to remove negative energy.

Cleromancy A method of divination by casting dice, sticks, stones, and other materials onto the ground.

Crystallomancy Another term for crystal ball reading—gazing into a crystal ball to receive insights and predictions for the future.

Dowsing The traditional method of using a forked piece of wood or a pendulum to locate underground water sources. Pendulum dowsing for divination purposes involves the use of a weighted object that hangs at the end of a chain, rope, or cord. The direction of the pendulum's swing provides "yes" or "no" answers to questions.

Grounding A practice that makes you feel present, centered, and balanced.

Hepatoscopy Inspecting the liver of an animal for divination purposes.

Palmistry Another term for palm reading—examining someone's palms to decipher their personality traits and predict their future. Also known as chiromancy.

Psychic A person who has the ability to read, see, or divine things that fall outside of the sphere of scientific knowledge.

Querent The person who is seeking guidance or answers from a divination method.

Reader The person who is performing the divination work—interpreting the messages and providing the reading to the querent.

Rebirth A type of spiritual awakening or transformation in which the person is renewed and ready for a fresh start in their life.

Reflexology A type of therapy based on the principle that particular parts of the foot correspond with specific body parts.

Scrying A form of divination performed by looking at a body of water, a crystal ball, a mirror, smoke, or ink in water to decipher messages.

Shamanism: Deeply rooted in nature, a practice in which the practitioner, known as a shaman, enters a trancelike state to interact with the spirit world, receive intuitive insights, and manifest healing.

Sixth sense An intuitive means of perception beyond the five basic senses of sight, smell, touch, taste, and hearing.

Smudging The method of burning bundles of herbs (often sage) and allowing the smoke to waft through areas and over items in need of cleansing.

Solestry Another term for foot reading—analyzing someone's foot size and shape to determine their personality and other influences that may affect the individual in the future.

Tasseomancy Divination by means of interpreting the shapes and patterns of tea leaves and coffee grounds.

Trigrams Ancient Chinese symbols formed of broken and unbroken lines, used in dice divination.

Visualization Forming an image of something in your mind.

Wheel of the Year A circular symbol used to outline the annual seasonal cycles and solar events celebrated by ancient civilizations, such as the Celts.

Index

Acknowledgments

I would like to acknowledge the wonderful team at CICO Books who are a delight to work with. In particular, my commissioning editor, Carmel Edmonds, and the amazing Imogen Valler-Miles who helped to make sense of my prose and shape the book with her expertise. I would also like to thank the design team who have done a brilliant job of bringing my words to life on the page.

Tarot and oracle decks featured in this book

From left to right, the tarot cards illustrated on pages 104–105 come from the following tarot decks: *Manifestation Tarot* by Jayne Wallace, illustrated by Julia Cellini; *Seasonal Power Tarot* by Leah Vanderveldt, illustrated by Emma Taylor; *The Mythical Creatures Tarot* by Jayne Wallace, illustrated by Julia Cellini; *The Moon & Stars Tarot* by Jayne Wallace, illustrated by Hannah Davies; *Magical Self-Care Tarot* by Leah Vanderveldt, illustrated by Emma Taylor; *Lunar Tarot* by Jayne Wallace, illustrated by Julia Cellini; *The Astrology Tarot* by Joanna Watters, illustrated by Bárbara Tamilin; *Elemental Power Tarot* by Melinda Lee Holm, illustrated by Rohan Daniel Eason.

The tarot cards illustrated on pages 106–115 come from *The Golden Tarot* by Liz Dean, illustrated by Melissa Launay.

From left to right, the oracle cards illustrated on page 120 come from the following oracle decks: *The Guardian Angel Oracle Deck* by Delia Ciccarelli, illustrated by Delia Ciccarelli; *The Celtic Goddess Oracle Deck* by Gillian Kemp, illustrated by Julia Cellini; *Bird Messages* by Susie Green, illustrated by Alan Weston.

All of the tarot and oracle decks listed above are published by CICO Books.

Picture credits

Crystal photography by Roy Palmer and Geoff Dann, all © CICO Books.

Illustrations by Michael Hill, Emma Taylor, Rosie Scott, Stephen Dew, Melissa Launay, Trina Dalziel, Tiffany Lynch, Bárbara Tamilin, and Delia Ciccarelli, all © CICO Books, except as listed below.

© Julia Cellini: p. 104 far left, p. 104 middle right, p. 105 middle left, p. 120 middle

© Hannah Davies: p. 104 far right

© Rohan Daniel Eason: p. 105 far right

© Alan Weston: p. 120 right

© Walaiporn Sangkeaw/Adobe Stock: p. 48, p. 51, p. 62, p. 64 (sticks)

© Isasoulart/Adobe Stock: pp. 86–87

© PawLoveArt/Adobe Stock and KPstudio/Adobe Stock: page borders and frames throughout